AF519753

Handbook for Project Control Professionals

A Practical Guide to Completing Projects on Time, Within the Budget and Meeting All Stakeholders' Expectations

Syed Ali Dilawer

ATLANTIC

PUBLISHERS & DISTRIBUTORS (P) LTD

Published by

ATLANTIC

PUBLISHERS & DISTRIBUTORS (P) LTD

7/22, Ansari Road, Darya Ganj,
New Delhi-110002
Phones : +91-11-40775252, 23273880, 23275880, 23280451
Fax : +91-11-23285873
Web : www.atlanticbooks.com
E-mail : orders@atlanticbooks.com

Branch Office
5, Nallathambi Street, Wallajah Road,
Chennai-600002
Phones : +91-44-64611085, 32413319
E-mail : chennai@atlanticbooks.com

Copyright © The Author, 2010

ISBN 978-81-269-1473-9

All rights reserved. No part of this publication may be reproduced, stored in a retrieval system, transmitted or utilized in any form or by any means, electronic, mechanical, photocopying, recording or otherwise, without the prior permission of the copyright owner. Application for such permission should be addressed to the publisher.

Printed in India at Nice Printing Press, A-33/3A, Site-IV, Industrial Area, Sahibabad, Ghaziabad, U.P.

Preface

"Predicting the future is easy, it's trying to figure out what's going on now that's hard."

—Fritz R.S. Dressler

This *Handbook* is the result of over 19 years of experience as a Project Management Professional. During the course of my experience, I have not come across any comprehensive handbook for Project Control Professionals, which has urged me to prepare this *Handbook*.

If we are going to control a project, we need to know two things: where we are supposed to be and where we are. The plan tells where we are supposed to be. As for where we actually are, it comes from the project information system.

This *Handbook* has been prepared by giving due consideration to practical requirements of Project Control Professionals. It provides a comprehensive, down-to-earth guide to every aspect of project and details the processes, workflows and procedures related to Project Control. Its purpose is to serve as a reference manual for Project Control Professionals as they work to make the process, a part of their daily operation.

Syed Ali Dilawer

Acknowledgements

It is impossible to individually acknowledge all the people who have contributed to this book over the years. My heartfelt thanks go to them. I am indebted to my wife, Naghma Shireen Syed for assisting me in writing this book and for her patience, love, and encouragement.

I am thankful to Atlantic Publishers & Distributors (P) Ltd. for evincing interest in publishing this book.

Syed Ali Dilawer

Contents

Units and Conversion

1

1.1 Metric Measurement Conversion

Symbol	When You Know	Multiply By	To Find	Symbol
LENGTH				
in.	inches	2.54	centimeters	cm
ft.	feet	30	centimeters	cm
yd.	yards	0.9	meters	m
mi.	miles	1.6	kilometers	km
mm	millimeters	0,04	inches	in
cm	centimeters	0.4	inches	in
m	meters	3.3	feet	ft
m	meters	1.1	yards	yd
km	kilometers	0.6	miles	mi.
AREA	**When You Know**	**Multiply By**	**To Find**	**Symbol**
in^2	square inches	6.5	sq. centimeter	cm^2
ft^2	square feet	0.09	square meters	m^2
yd^2	square yards	0.8	square meters	m^2
mi^2	square miles	2.58	sq. kilometers	km^2
	acres	0.4	hectares	ha
cm^2	sq. centimeters	0.16	square inches	in^2
m^2	square meters	1.2	square yards	yd^2
km^2	sq. kilometers	0.4	square miles	mi^2
ha	hectares (10,000 m^2)	2.5	acres	
WEIGHT	**When You Know**	**Multiply By**	**To Find**	**Symbol**
oz.	ounces	28	grams	g
lb.	pounds	0.45	kilograms	kg
	short tons (2000 lbs.)	0.9	tons	t
	long tons (2240 lbs.)	1.01	tons	t

WEIGHT	When You Know	Multiply By	To Find	Symbol
g	grams	0.035	ounce	oz.
kg	kilograms	2.2	pounds	lb.
t	tons (1000 kg)	1.1	short tons	
t	tons (1000 kg)	0.98	long tons	

VOLUME	When You Know	Multiply By	To Find	Symbol
tsp.	Teaspoons	5	milliliters	ml
tbsp.	Tablespoons	15	milliliters	ml
fl. oz.	fluid ounces	30	milliliters	ml
c	cups	0.24	liters	l
pt.	Pints	0.47	liters	l
qt.	quarts	0.95	liters	l
gal.	gallons (U.S.)	3.8	liters	l
gal.	gallons (Imp.)	4.5	liters	l
ft^3	cubic feet	.028	cubic meters	m^3
yd^3	cubic yards	0.76	cubic meters	m^3
ml	milliliters	0.03	fluid ounces	fl. oz.
l	liters	2.1	pints	pt.
l	liters	1.0	quarts	qt.
l	liters	0.2	gallons (U.S.)	gal (U.S.)

VOLUME	When You Know	Multiply By	To Find	Symbol
l	liters	0.22	gallons (Imp.)	gal (Imp.)
m^3	cubic meters	35	cubic feet	ft^3
m^3	cubic meters	1.3	cubic yards	yd^3

TEMPERATURE

$$°C = (°F - 32) \times .555$$

$$°F = (°C \times 1.8) + 32$$

Project Control Overview

2

2.1 INTRODUCTION

A project is "a unique endeavour to produce a set of deliverables within clearly specified time, cost and quality constraints".

The only truly successful project is the one that delivers what is supposed to get results and meets stakeholder expectations.

Project Control is exercised by comparing progress against planned performance and taking steps to correct for any deviation from the proper course. Project Controls provide the capability to reveal trends toward cost overrun and/or schedule slippage. Identifying those trends early enables more successful project management and reduced risk.

Effective project control requires effective project planning, scheduling and cost control, risk management procedures to be established using carefully defined process and document controls, metrics, performance indicators and forecasting.

Relationship between Project Management and Controls

Project management is aggregated into five groups, defined as the Project Management process groups:

- Initiating process—authorizing the project or phase
- Planning process—defining and refining objectives and selecting the best of the alternative courses
- Executing process—coordinating people and other resources to carry out the plan
- Controlling process—ensuring that project objectives are met by monitoring and measuring progress regularly, to identify variances from plan so that corrective action can be taken when necessary
- Closing process—formalizing acceptance of the project or phase and bringing it to an orderly end

The Project Management Processes are not discrete, one-time events; they are overlapping activities that occur at varying levels of intensity throughout each phase of the project.

Effective control of the project is more likely to be achieved with a well defined set of controls in place. The purpose of this section is to provide uniform and integrated approach to all aspects of project control as it is applied throughout the planning, procurement, fabrication and construction phases of project execution.

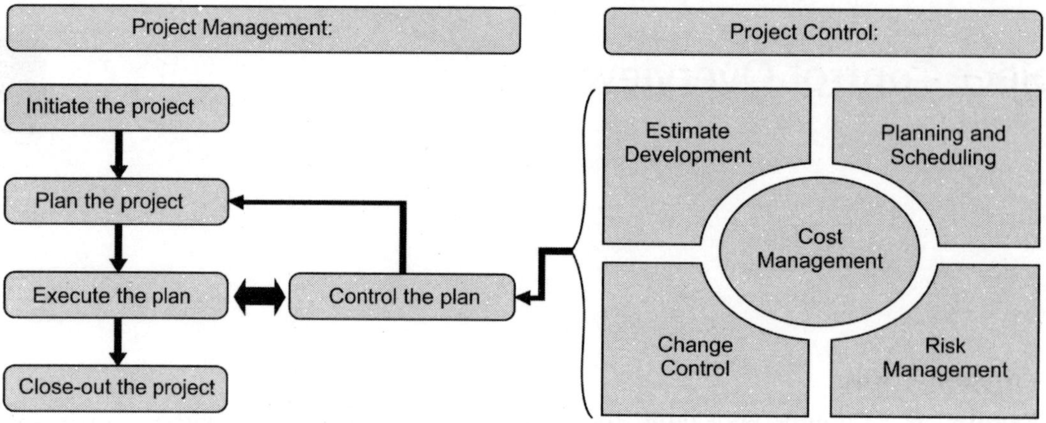

Fig. 2.1: Relationship between Project Management and Controls

The book covers in detail the following key areas of project control:

- Project Control Overview
- Project Execution Plan
- Work Breakdown Structure
- Planning and Scheduling
- Commercial Management
- Value Engineering
- Change Management
- Progress Measurement
- Risk Management
- Communication Management
- Earned Value Management
- Quality Control and Assurance
- Comparison Between Standard Form of Construction Contract
- Delay and Disruption/Project Close-out
- Productivity Norms
- Progress Reporting

"Unless you know both cost and schedule, you have absolutely no idea where your project actually stands."

Project Execution Plan

3

3.1 INTRODUCTION

The Project Execution Plan (PEP) is a live document that sets out the project scope, defines the management health and safety expectations, describes the procurement and construction plans for the development, provides information of the project organization and structure, and gives the project team a clear understanding of project budgets and cost plans associated with the activity undertaken.

The PEP does not replace or initiate any agreement, engagement or contract that may already exist between the Client and any other organization.

This is a "live" document and is to be amended and developed regularly throughout the project period to reflect changes to objectives, plans, costs or organization.

Every project shall have a PEP prepared and approved not later than three calendar weeks after contract award notification, or earlier if so directed by the Management contract.

Benefits

Focused Team—The PEP provides the framework for the Project Team to understand the project organization, the communication structure and the controls and procedures which will be used to manage the Project. This results in better cohesion between the team members, the management and the client.

Best Practice—Developing PEP is industry's best practice and as such shows Clients that organization works at the highest level of project management. This raises organization marketability and will bring new Clients through the adoption of such practices.

Associated Risk of NOT Following Procedure

If PEP is not prepared or not followed, then there will be no framework for the Project Team to understand the scope, project costs, communication structure, controls and procedures, etc. which will be used to manage the Project. If team members are forced to discover this information for themselves, it is unlikely that discovery will yield the same results leading to confusion and inaccurate reporting.

3.2 CONTENTS

Section	Title	Rev 0	Rev 1	Rev 2	Reason for Latest Revisions
1.0	Introduction				
2.0	Definitions				
3.0	Clients Brief and Vision				
4.0	Procurement Strategy				
5.0	Budget				
6.0	Program				
7.0	Risk				
8.0	Contractor Report				
9.0	Project Organisation				
10.0	Responsibilities Matrix				
11.0	Meetings				
12.0	Procedures				
Appendix A	Change Control Procedure				
Appendix B	Master Program				
Appendix C	Project Risk Register				
Appendix D	Project Organisational Chart				
Appendix E	Project Directory				
Appendix F	Drawings/Specification Issue				

"We must now determine all the steps that will get us there."

Work Breakdown Structure (WBS)

4

4.1 INTRODUCTION

Successful Project Management relies on thorough planning. This begins by defining the project objectives with sufficiently detailed information. The Work Breakdown Structure (WBS) provides the foundation for defining work as it relates to project objectives. The WBS also establishes the framework for managing the work to its completion.

A WBS, a deliverable-oriented hierarchical decomposition of the work to be executed by the project team to accomplish the project objectives and create the required deliverable.

The WBS provides the foundation for integrating the work package and intermediate deliverables with all other aspects of project initiation, planning, execution, monitoring and controlling, and closing.

A deliverable-oriented WBS provides many benefits to the project, including the following:

- Better communication to project sponsors, stakeholders and team members.
- More accurate estimation of tasks, risks, timelines and costs.
- Separating project deliverable into component parts to ensure the project plan matches the approved project scope and will fulfill the overall objectives of the project.
- Increase confidence that 100% of the work is identified and included.
- A foundation for the control process within the project.
- Decomposes (or disassembles) the overall project scope into deliverables and supports the definition of the work effort required for effective management.

The 100% Rule

The 100% rule is a core characteristic of the WBS. This rule states that the WBS includes 100% of the work defined by the project scope and captures ALL deliverables—internal, external, and interim in terms of work to be completed, including project related management. The 100% rule is one of the most important principles guiding the development, decomposition and evaluation of the WBS. The role applies at all levels within the hierarchy.

The WBS should not include any work that falls outside the actual scope of the project, that is, it cannot include more than 100% of the work.

Representation of the WBS

The WBS can be represented in a variety of ways including graphical, textual, or tabular views. Regardless of the representation used, the WBS enables the project team to predict and forecast costs, schedules, resource requirements, and allocations more accurately.

4.2 PROBLEM DIAGNOSTIC CHECKLIST

The following are representative examples of major project problems resulting from key WBS defects:

- There are frequently missed deadlines and an extended schedule:
  - Have all major and minor deliverables been included? Failure to include all deliverables within the initial WBS can increase project schedules when missed deliverables are identified.
  - Have deliverables been defined specifically enough to allow for appropriate work packages to be developed?
  - Does the WBS facilitate the use of Earned Value Management techniques?
- Project is over budget:
  - Does the WBS provide logical summary points for assessing accomplishments, as well as for measuring costs and schedule performance?
  - Does the WBS facilitate the use of Earned Value Management techniques?
- Individuals are unable to use the new product or feature:
  - Are deliverables decomposed into smaller, more specific deliverables? For example, a deliverable of training might not be decomposed thoroughly enough to cover all of the people who need training to use the new product, process, or service.
  - Are the WBS elements deliverable-focused?
  - Were appropriate assembly or integration deliverables and testing activities present?
  - Were training and implementation deliverables defined?
- The project scope has changed and is unmanageable:
  - Has a WBS been created for the project?
  - Does the WBS decompose the overall project scope into deliverables?
  - Does the WBS provide a level of flexibility for change?
  - Has the WBS been updated when necessary changes are approved by the change control process?
  - Has the WBS been placed under change control?
- The project has become an ongoing project with no end in sight:
  - Has a maintenance plan been developed for post implementation if needed?
  - Does the project have a specific end point?
  - Does the WBS include a close-out phase or plan?
  - Is the endeavour actually a project or is it an ongoing operation?

- Project team members are confused about their individual responsibilities:
  - Do the WBS elements define overlapping responsibilities for the creation of a deliverable?
  - Is the information within the WBS at the appropriate level of detail and in communication processes and decision authorities agreed upon beforehand?
  - Do the WBS elements reflect work with specific, tangible deliverables?
  - Have all key stakeholders, including subject matter experts, contributed to the creation and validation of the WBS?
- Some planned work does not get done:
  - Has all required work been included in the WBS?
  - Are the WBS elements deliverable-focused?
  - Has the WBS organized around deliverable rather than process steps?
  - Was decomposition completed before dependencies and durations were defined?

4.3 THINGS TO CONSIDER WHEN PREPARING A WBS

A high level WBS can often be developed early in the conceptual stage of the project. Once the project is defined and specifications are prepared, a more detailed WBS can then be developed.

The following list of questions should be considered when developing a WBS to manage a project:

- Is the project scope statement defined and issued?
- Has the project scope statement been defined and issued?
- Has the Project Manager and the team formulated a vision of the final product(s), services, or results?
- Has personnel who will do the work been assigned to develop the WBS?
- What project are the project's component parts?
- How do the pieces work together?
- What needs to be done?
- Have the project's intended business objectives been defined? What is required to achieve the business value?
- Has the entire project been thought through? Have the high-level deliverables been progressively decomposed?
- Have all deliverables, both interim and final, been identified? What is to be provided? What is required?
- Has the relationship of each component to the end product been defined? What methods will be employed? What special processes will be needed? What are the quality requirements? What kinds of inspections need to be done?
- Have the activities that are needed to support the deliverables been identified, including those that directly or indirectly facilitate their creation?

- Does the project require any external sources to contribute to the project and have they been identified?
- Has all work associated with risk management been identified? Have risks associated with project assumptions been identified?

These thoughts and questions are intended to help the Project Manager develop a clear statement of what the product(s) of the project are. Once completed, all of the work packages (i.e., the lowest-level WBS elements) should together comprise the complete list of deliverables for the project.

4.4 GUIDANCE IN CHOOSING A METHOD FOR PREPARING A WBS

In developing a WBS, the project management team needs to decide first which development method to use. Some guidelines and explanations for which approach might be more appropriate are as follows:

Top-Down

Use the top-down in this situation:

- The Project Manager and Project Management Team have little to experience in developing Work Breakdown Structures. Top-down development allows for progressive understanding and elaboration on of the WBS.

Bottom-Up

Use the bottom-up approach in these situations:

- The nature of the projects, the project team might already have a very good understanding of all interim deliverables required for the new project.
- The nature of the project life cycle is well known. If the organization always uses the same project life cycle, the interim deliverables for that life cycle are well known and can be used to begin bottom-up WBS development.
- Appropriate WBS templates are available. If the organization has WBS from projects with similar products or services, and these can be reused, a bottom-up approach enhances the team's ability to customize the WBS template.

WBS Standards and Templates

There are plenty of sample WBS available in the literature, but the choice to use sample WBS as templates must be made carefully. The organization can have WBS templates for very similar projects, and the use of these templates is highly encouraged. However, if the project significantly differs from other projects in the organization, and no template seems to apply, develop the WBS from scratch with a top-down approach.

Iterations

Construction of the WBS is an iterative process and may rely on more than one method to produce the final high quality WBS. For example, a WBS template and the top-down approach may be used initially to determine the overall structure of the WBS, while it might be more appropriate to use the bottom-up method to verify that all the elements are present to achieve a particular deliverable.

4.5 GENERAL FACTORS TO BE CONSIDERED

In developing a WBS, the following basic tenets should be considered:

- Each WBS element represents a single tangible or intangible deliverable.
- Deliverables include both final and interim deliverables that are required to create the final results.
- Deliverables include intangible items, such as information/communication, integration, administration, training, process management, and procurement.
- All deliverables are explicitly included in the WBS.
- Deliverables are unique and distinct.
- All significant reporting mechanisms, such as review meetings, monthly reports and test reports are included and identified in the WBS.
- Clearly defining the project deliverables, so that each is unique, ensures there will be no duplication in the outcomes of the project or of the work performed to produce the end-products.
- Accountability for each work package can be assigned to a single project team member or subcontractor. If this is not possible, then reconsider whether or not the work package can be further decomposed.
- Each element in the WBS representing subcontracted or externally committed deliverables directly corresponds to matching elements in the subcontractor's WBS.
- The deliverables are logically decomposed to the level that represents how they will be produced and managed (e.g. designed, purchased, subcontracted, or fabricated).
- All WBS elements are compatible with organizational and accounting structures.

The following basic guidelines should be considered when organizing WBS elements into the WBS hierarchy:

- Each WBS element belongs to only one parent WBS element.
- The set of child elements into which a parent element is decomposed includes all of the work contained in the parent, such that the 100% Rule applies.
- A coding scheme is used for WBS elements that clearly represent the hierarchical structure when viewed in text format.
- All "legs" of the WBS need not be to the same depths. Some areas of the WBS will need to show more detail than others.
- There is no need to have all work packages at the same level.
- The WBS development process should:
  - Be iterative.
  - Be reviewed and revised as the rest of the project planning process progresses.
- Provide a vehicle for flexibility, particularly when the scope of the project effort might change.

4.6 SELECTION OF THE TYPE OF WBS ELEMENT TO BE INCLUDED

A WBS organizes and defines the total work scope of the project. Not every WBS, however, needs to include all types of work. Rather, the kinds of work included in a WBS should be dictated by the scope and nature of the project for which the WBS is being developed.

Structuring the Logic of the Decomposition:

> An essential feature of a WBS is that it clearly and comprehensively defines the scope of the project work through decomposition of deliverables into a hierarchy of simpler components, thereby providing one of the primary methods for managing complex projects. The way that the Project Manager decomposes the project (i.e., the logic used for decomposing the work) can vary depending on the needs and requirements of the performing organization and the use to which the WBS will be put.

It is important that the WBS remain deliverable-oriented, rather than process-oriented, and explicitly contains all intermediate deliverables.

4.7 WBS STRUCTURE GUIDELINES

The contents of this section reflect a view of recognised standards for the development of Work Breakdown Structures customised to meet the needs of the projects.

These are, as stated, guidelines only, and the WBS for a specific should be structured to meet the needs of that project, but should still aim to align with these guidelines. In addition WBS designs must be reviewed and agreed with the head of planning and Project Manager.

WBS guidelines for multiphase projects

The proposed WBS guidelines for a multiphase consists of 6 levels as follows:

Level 1: Program Name
Example: XXX, etc.

Level 2: Project
Example: Infrastructure, or Zones

Level 3: Area of Work
Example: Plot no., phase

Level 4: Type of Work
Example: Engineering, Interfaces, Procurement, NOCs, Construction

Level 5: Area Details
Example: Golf, Marina, etc. for area detail

Level 6: Work Details
Example: Scheme design, detail design, civil work, finishing work, etc.

WBS guidelines for single phase projects

Level 1: Project
Example: Infrastructure, or Zones

Level 2: Area of Work

Example: Plot no., phase

Level 3: Project Stages

Stage 0—Master Planning

Stage 1—Concept Design Stage

Stage 2—Schematic Design Stage

Stage 3—Detail Design Stage

Stage 4—Final Design and Tendering Docs

Stage 5, 6—Tendering/Award

Stage 7—Construction

OR

Type of Work

Example: Engineering, Interfaces, Procurement, NOCs, Construction

Level 4: Area Details

Example: Golf, Marina, etc. for area detail

Level 5: Work Details

Example: Scheme design, detail design, civil work, finishing work, etc.

"Identifies all the work to be performed—if it is not in the WBS it is not part of the project."

4.8 WBS SAMPLE

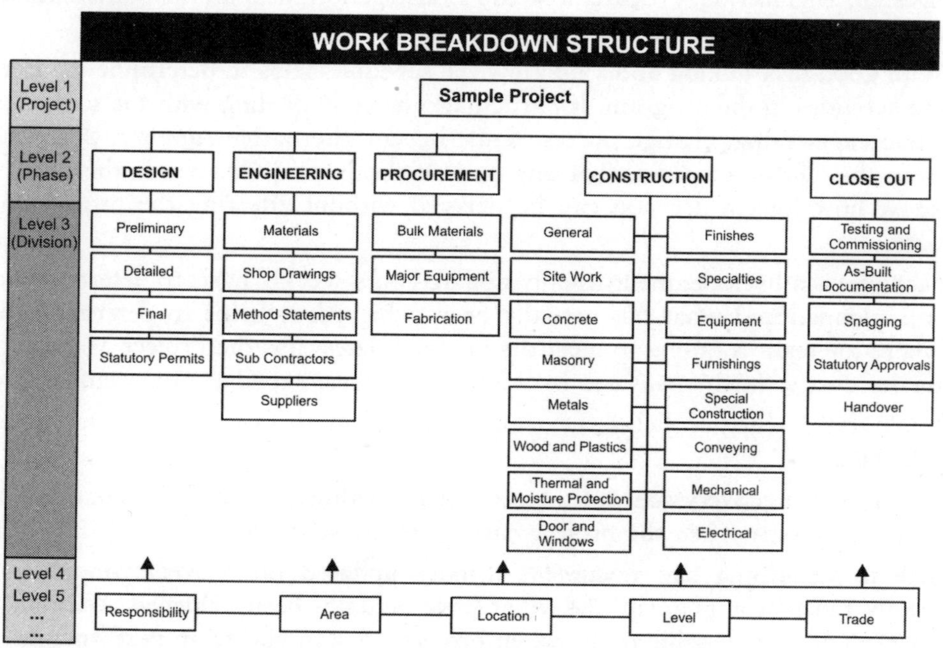

Project Scheduling

5

5.1 INTRODUCTION

There are three objectives in the Project Scheduling System:

- To identify a scheme for achieving prescribed goals through the development of a well-defined and realistic plan.
- To provide a visual means of conveying the information contained in this plan to all levels of management.
- To facilitate timely updating and monitoring procedures as necessary.

The Schedule is a document which links the scope of work, budget, resources, etc. in a time phased manner. Without a schedule it would not be possible to establish at any point of time how much work should have been completed or how much cost should have been expended. It is the starting point for any Project Controls effort.

- Schedule determines critical path(s) which derives the project completion date or any other milestones. This helps the Project Manager to ensure that various departments (Design, Engineering, Procurement and Construction) deal all the matters related to the activities on critical path as a top priority.
- With good task linking and logic flow the schedule helps to determine the criticality of the activities in the program. It particularly helps in dealing with the scenarios such as value engineering, change orders, tendering an alternative supplier, decision awaited from the Client, suspension of any part of the works, etc. where the team wants to know how long a decision can be delayed without effecting the project completion date.
- Schedule is a live document usually updated on a weekly basis to determine how much was planned and what has actually been achieved. It helps to determine the area(s) where the team is failing to meet the planned dates thus the Project Manager can take the necessary timely measures by adding resources, expedite procurement, etc.
- Look-ahead schedule helps the team to establish short-term goals from the master schedule.
  - Revised, Recovery schedule, accelerated schedule, "What If" scenarios, etc. are all possible only when the project has a baseline schedule.

Schedule is actually a live document usually updated on a weekly/monthly basis to determine how much was planned and what have actually been achieved. Without having a Schedule in place it is impossible to ascertain project's health and team performance.

5.2 DIFFERENT TYPES OF SCHEDULES

For management of the Project, the following Schedules are developed:

- Master Schedule
- Project Schedules
- Revised Schedules
- Recovery Schedules
- Special Schedules

Master Schedule

At the outset of the project, the Project Manager prepares a Master Schedule that integrates the Design, Procurement and Construction phases of the Project. This shall be further broken down to the various packages that constitute the Project.

Once the scheduling objectives for both the short- and long-term have been agreed upon, the Project completion date is determined and "locked in". The Master Schedule thus developed shall be the 'Baseline' for comparison with updated actual data and will be the basis for developing more detailed schedules for individual trade packages.

The Master Schedule is updated periodically with actual data to compare against the baseline. Revisions to the Master Schedule shall be made in case of changes in design, design schedule, package strategy, etc.

As the design and procurement phases progress, on the basis of the Master Schedule, the Project Manager develops schedules with reasonable detail to demonstrate the feasibility and strategy for executing the project within the constraints of the approved Master Schedule. The objectives of such an exercise shall be to:

- Identify the sequence of works for execution.
- Determine the inter-relationships (FS, SS, SF, FF) between activities forming the Schedule.
- Analyze and Establish interface constraints between different trades.
- Form a framework within which the execution of Project should proceed.

This enables to produce indicative schedules for individual trade packages and establish interim Milestone Dates within those schedules. Once the 'Schedule of Works' of any trade package Contractor is finalized, the detailed schedule of that trade package is removed from the PM's Schedule. However, the Project Manager will update the progress of each trade package on his Master Schedule, which will be in a summary form, based on update information provided by the Contractor.

Project Schedules

- Review the Project Scope of Work
- Review the Project Execution Plan
- Review the WBS developed
- Establish the level of reporting and coding structure in P3/P6 (Primavera Project Planner)/Any other planning software
- Enter all activities into P3/P6/Any other planning software

- Obtain a copy of the Project Estimate
- Enter the estimated man-hours against the activities into P3/P6 of any other planning software
- Discuss with the discipline engineers, the crew size for each activity, to establish the activity duration
- Discuss and establish with Discipline Engineer, the logic links between activities
- Discuss and establish logic links between disciplines
- Run a time analysis (first pass) to check end date against Contract Completion date
- Make adjustments to durations and logic to maintain Contract Completion Date
- Print the detailed schedule, manpower histograms and planned progress "S" curves for comments
- Code activities to enable the various levels of summary schedules to be produced
- Incorporate all comments
- Issue schedule for approval by the Project Manager and issue to Client
- Incorporate any comments received from the Client
- Re-issue Project Schedule for issue to Client

At this stage, the mutually agreed Project Schedule is also called as "Baseline Schedule". This schedule is frozen as a target schedule in P3/P6/Any other planning software and a copy of the same is used for subsequent updates.

The Client or Client Rep shall require all participants, including the Design Consultant and the Construction Contractors to submit their Project schedules or detailed schedules of their relevant activities while at the same time abide by the several milestones and constraints set by the Client.

To ensure reasonable compatibility and reduce the problems of collecting, organizing and reporting the information in a regular, coordinated manner, the format and structure of all schedule information and reports submitted by any party to the Project is specified by the Client or Client Rep and is a part of the contract documents.

Revised Schedules

If, at any time:

Actual progress is too slow to complete within the Time for Completion or progress has fallen (or will fall) behind the current program and/or changes in scope work, the Client may instruct the Contractor to submit a revised program and supporting report describing the revised methods.

Recovery Schedules

In the event that the project completion has been delayed, a recovery schedule must be prepared and issued to the Client, for review and approval.

Prior to the issue of the recovery schedule, certain questions must be asked:

- Who is responsible for the delay?
- Can the delay be covered by a Change Order?

- What is the cost impact of the recovery schedule?
- Are there Liquidated Damages involved?
- Review cost of recovery against LDs (Liquid Damages).
- Can the schedule be recovered?

After asking all the above questions, a recovery plan must be established; this plan will be reflected in the recovery schedule. Development of the recovery plan is as follows:

- Review the critical path activities and discuss with the Discipline Engineer's methods to reduce durations in line with the recovery execution plan.
- Review the critical path to check for logic errors or potential changes in the logic to recover the overall project duration.
- Review progress reports to highlight unproductive working methods.
- Review manning levels. Are they realistic and within the budget?
- Highlight activities that will be undertaken by working extended hours or shift system.
- Incorporate all comments and policies established in the recovery execution plan.
- Issue the recovery schedule for review and comments.
- Issue approved schedule to the Client.
- Incorporate Client's comments.
- Issue recovery schedule for Client approval.

Special Schedules

Special Schedule can be one of the following:

- Sub-contract schedule
- Shut-down schedule
- Detailed vendor erection schedule
- Change Order fragnet
- Delay analysis
- Intermediate recovery schedule

The procedure for development of these special schedules is basically the same for producing any schedule, with the exception that more detail is usually required; and therefore, more involvement by the Discipline Engineer or specialist.

In the case of the Change Order fragnet, all disciplines will be involved:

- Create a sub-project within the main project schedule that will contain the special schedule.
- Obtain all the information required to prepare the schedule.
- Prepare a scope of work for the schedule, issue to all parties for comments.
- Prepare the schedule independent of the main schedule, to ensure all activities are captured.
- Issue the schedule to all parties for review and comments.

- Enter logic links between the special schedule and main schedule, to determine any impact on the overall schedule.
- In the event of an impact on the overall schedule, highlight the extent and location of impact and if possible, the cost impact.

"If you have no plan, you can't possibly have control."

5.3 PLANNING CYCLE

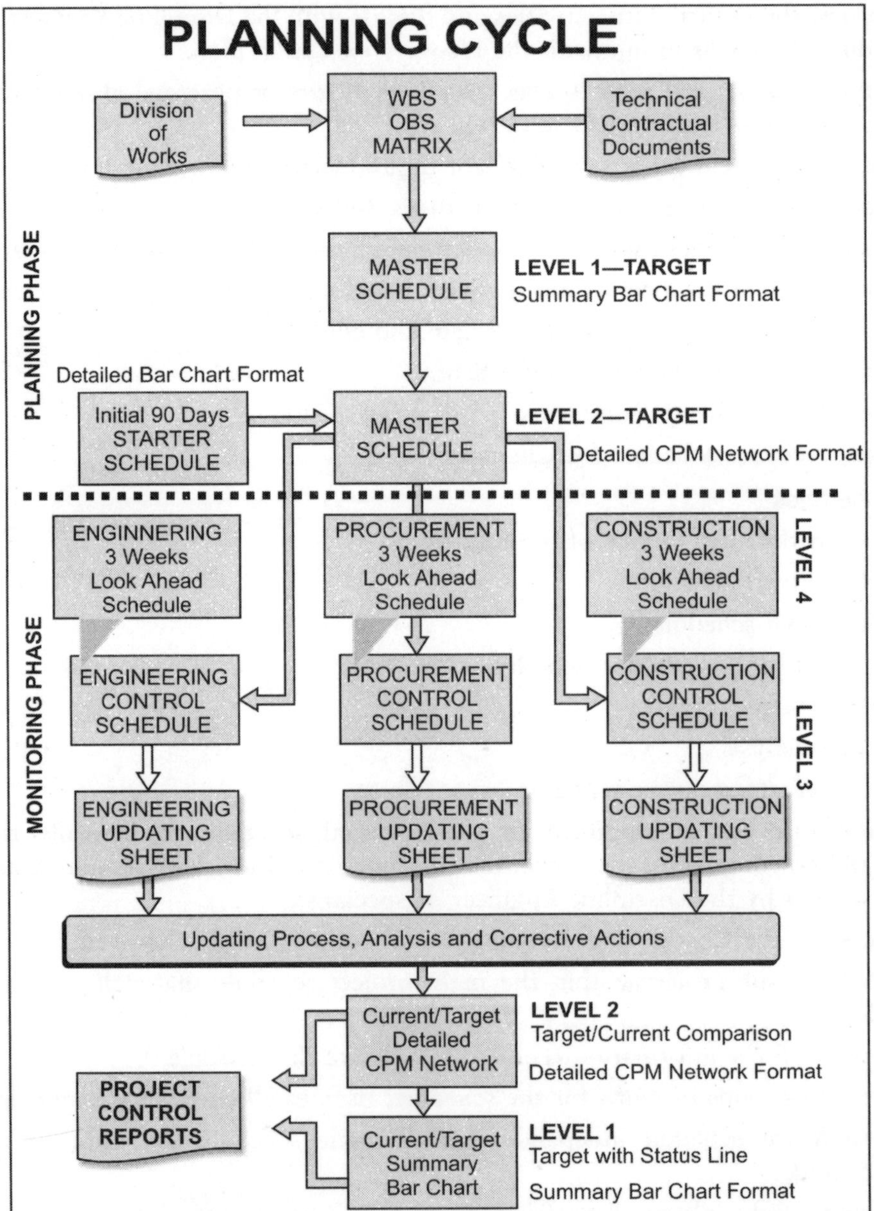

Commercial Management

6

6.1 INTRODUCTION

The term Cost Management, when applied to a project, describes the activities required to monitor, control and report on the costs of a project, and also to value and apply for payment for completed work.

It is important at this point to draw the distinction between a "budget" and an "estimate". Estimates are the result of developing an approximation of the costs of the resources needed to complete project activities.

A "budget" is an accumulation and allocation of the overall cost estimates to individual activities or work packages to establish a cost baseline for measuring project performance. Reality may dictate that estimates are accomplished after budgetary approval is provided, but estimates should be done prior to budget request wherever possible.

In summary terms, the budget is set by the Owner very early in the project life cycle and it reflects the amount of money he has allotted for the complete works. This budget may have been developed purely on conceptual design.

As the design progresses, the every detailed information allows "estimates" of the completed works to be developed until the design is complete and the "cost control baseline" is developed against the completed design.

The baseline should not exceed the budget, or the budget should be increased to allow for the more precise estimate. Thereafter, performance is measured against the baseline.

6.2 COST PLANNING

Cost Planning describes the process of estimating the cost of a project at each design stage. As the design is developed through the feasibility, outline/concept, scheme and detail design stages; more information becomes available and more detailed cost estimates may be accomplished.

Further development of the cost estimate is linked to the design deliverable dates whereby meaningful stages of the design can be properly assessed and appropriate actions taken. At each stage, they must be approved by the Client/Owner.

On completion of the detail design, the Client must approve the Elemental Cost Plan, which contains the costs of the individual building elements. The Project Cost Plan, or Initial Cost Plan, evolves from it by allocating each elemental cost to a work package. The approval of the Initial Cost Plan by the Client is defined as the Commitment Date.

The Initial Cost Plan forms the baseline cost control against which the financial performance of the project is measured. The costs recorded in it are not changed during the remainder of the project.

Scope and change control procedures are implemented and any cost variations are reported in the Adjusted Cost Plan and Estimated Final Cost or the Anticipated Total Cost.

6.3 ELEMENTAL COST PLAN

Throughout the period leading to the commitment date, in conjunction with the Client and the PM Team members, the Cost Consultant must prepare and submit for approval, an estimate structured by element. The estimate structured by element, or Elemental Cost Plan, must be distributed to the Client and the project team concurrently.

All estimating assumptions together with documents relied upon in establishing the conceptual estimate, must be set forth explicitly as material used for reference. Recipients must comment, in writing, within an agreed period, normally one or two weeks. The Cost Consultant must resolve and incorporate any required changes into the Elemental Cost Plan prior to its next issue.

The Elemental Cost Plan must contain an estimate by element, and further breakdown, by sub-element, together with a breakdown of fixed and reimbursable preliminaries.

6.4 INITIAL COST PLAN

Following the development of the list of Tender Packages, the Consultant in conjunction with the PM Team must reformat the Elemental Cost Plan into an Initial Cost Plan. The Initial Cost Plan must be submitted to the Client for approval. Prior to the commitment date, the package codes may be reformatted, as deemed necessary. Notification of the amended package codes must be issued, in writing, to the Client and the Design Consultants.

6.5 COST CONTROL BASELINE ESTIMATE

During the design stage, the PM Team is to review the Owner's budget, to monitor the budget throughout design and construction, and to report monthly (at a minimum) to the Owner, the current status of budgets. PM Team will also complete a detailed review of the Consultant's BOQ to ensure accuracy of take-offs and unit pricing.

The objectives of Cost Control during design are:

- Establish a realistic budget for the project in its entirety. The budget will be broken down into as much detail as possible.
- Monitor the costs (via the consultant's BOQ) against the budget to ensure that the project remains within the Owner's budget parameters.
- Ensure that no "surprises" arise during tendering that will require redesign to reduce cut costs.
- Ensure that the project comes in at or below the budget estimate.

The strategy to be employed for Cost Control is to keep very close control over the Design Professional's design. This will require the Consultant prepare and submit interim BOQ's for PM Team review at regular intervals during the design effort. In addition, PM Team will review all material and equipment selections with the Owner to ensure that the quality of the materials, and the overall design, are in keeping with Owner objectives for the project. Cost control strategies will also include:

- The target investment level prepared during the planning stage of the Development project and its sub-components will be prepared and approved by Client management. This will serve as the ceiling to which the projects' scope, quality, safety and schedule must be attained by. The investment level will be realistic.
- Validation Estimates is one of the methods to control the design/scope of the Project. PM team will establish procedures that require the Design Professional to design the scope of work and required quality standards to the available budget. To ensure that the Design Professionals are not over-designing, a validation estimate will be performed at the completion of schematic, design development and construction document phase.
- Completion of design prior to tender: Once a scope of work has been issued for tender to general Contractors, the design will be considered frozen and any changes will be tracked very carefully.

Budget Formulation and Monitoring

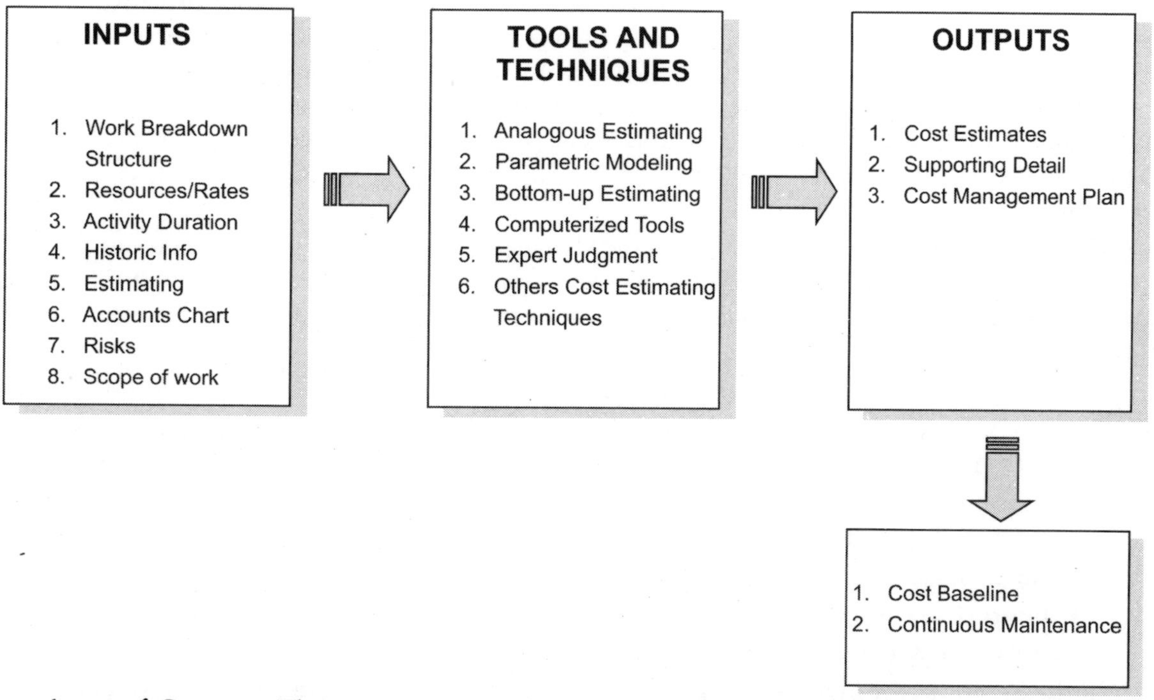

Areas of Concern: There are two primary areas of concern during design for cost control: (a) that the BOQ is relatively accurate in both measurements and estimated unit pricing, and (b) that the design be in accordance with Owner objectives and the project budget.

Benefits to Owner: The benefits that accrue to Client from design cost control are the delivery of a design that meets your requirements and that is within the budget parameters for the project.

6.6 THE CONTROL ESTIMATE

Preliminary Estimates

Preliminary estimates assist the overall cost-control program by serving as the first check against the budget, and by indicating cost overruns early enough for the project team to review the design for possible alternates. Since preliminary estimates are made prior to the completion of detail drawings, the margin for error is usually greater than for 'fair-cost' estimates.

Consequently, a larger contingency should be applied; this will vary with the amount of design information available and the extent of cost information obtainable from similar projects.

For phased construction program, it is especially important to prepare preliminary estimates by contract package. By comparing actual contract awards with the preliminary estimate, a running total of the current status of the project is available. Indicated overruns can stimulate revision of the criteria for later work packages in order to preserve overall budgets.

Fair-cost Estimates

Fair-cost Estimates are best prepared from the actual bid documents provided to the bidders. Whenever possible, it is helpful to complete the fair-cost estimate well before receiving bids so that any discrepancies in plans and specifications, duplications in scope, and possible value-engineering alternates suggested by the estimator can be communicated to the bidders via addendum before bids are received. In the event of a major difference from the preliminary estimates, this lead time is always helpful so that an intensive review of possible alternates can be started.

Fair-cost Estimates represent the Project Manager's appraisal of the fair value of the bid package to the owner. Local conditions, such as materials prices, wage rates, labour productivity, and anticipated competition, are important in achieving a reasonable estimate for the area.

Fair-cost Estimates in an integrated cost-progress control system will also develop significant additional information for upgrading the usefulness and accuracy of the schedule and progress-control portion of the overall control system. Some of these items include the following:

- An estimate of total man-hours of field effort required
- Estimated quantities for major items
- An estimate of reasonable unit costs for various components of the works
- Information for allocation of contract costs for owner capitalization and tax considerations (if applicable).

In the event, actual bids differ significantly from the fair-cost estimate, the PM Team can often meet with the low bidder and compare quantities and scope. Many times this comparison can pinpoint the reason for the discrepancy. Decisions regarding award, modifications, or rejection of bids will be greatly assisted if the PM Team has prepared a careful fair-cost estimate, separately itemizing labour, materials, and equipment costs in a manner similar to that of the bidding Contractor.

This estimate can be of great value to the field Project Manager in scheduling work, in reviewing change order requests, and in determining manpower requirements.

Definitive Estimates

Definitive estimates fix the anticipated cost of the project with little margin for error. As contracts are bid on a phased construction program, the overall estimated cost becomes more certain. When 90 per cent of the contracts have been awarded, less contingency is required than at the 50 per cent level. When 100 per cent of the contracts have been awarded, contingency is generally limited to providing for plan changes due to interference or error, for omissions or conflicts, or for other business risks inherent in the project.

Cost Control Baseline

As inferred above, progressive tender awards toward the point where 100 per cent of the packages are under agreed contract, yields a cost control baseline against which to measure progress and productivity.

As each tender package is awarded, the agreed construction contract price is compared to the owner's 'budget' for that works item to determine the design variance.

Thereafter, the awarded price becomes the cost control baseline.

This separation of design-tender cost estimate variances and the construction phase variances allows analysis of productivity of each element of the works.

During the construction phase, the cost of design errors and omissions may be included in the design variance in order to apportion the cost increases to correct causes and responsible entities.

6.7 COST REPORT SUMMARIES

Cost Report Summaries describe the actual and forecast status of the project; they generally commence with the preliminary estimate and end when the project is complete and all claims, if any, have been settled. In a normal program, cost reports showing estimated cost-at-completion can be prepared from the committed cost plus estimated costs-to-complete for the various contracts involved.

Some owners prefer that the PM Team perform additional accounting for recorded costs when these are paid as progress payments. Others prefer to handle this phase themselves and are interested in the PM Team report only to cover total commitments to date and estimated costs to complete. Similarly, some owners require continual cash-flow projections to accompany the cost reports, while others prefer to handle these themselves.

6.8 REPORTING SYSTEMS

Whether, with an automated cost reporting system or by spreadsheet program, the following cost categories must be indicated and calculated:

- Budget
- Budget changes
- Baseline (Committed, Contracted)
- Variations
- Actual cost to date
- Estimated cost to complete
- Estimated final cost at completion

6.9 BID DECISION PROCESS FLOW CHART

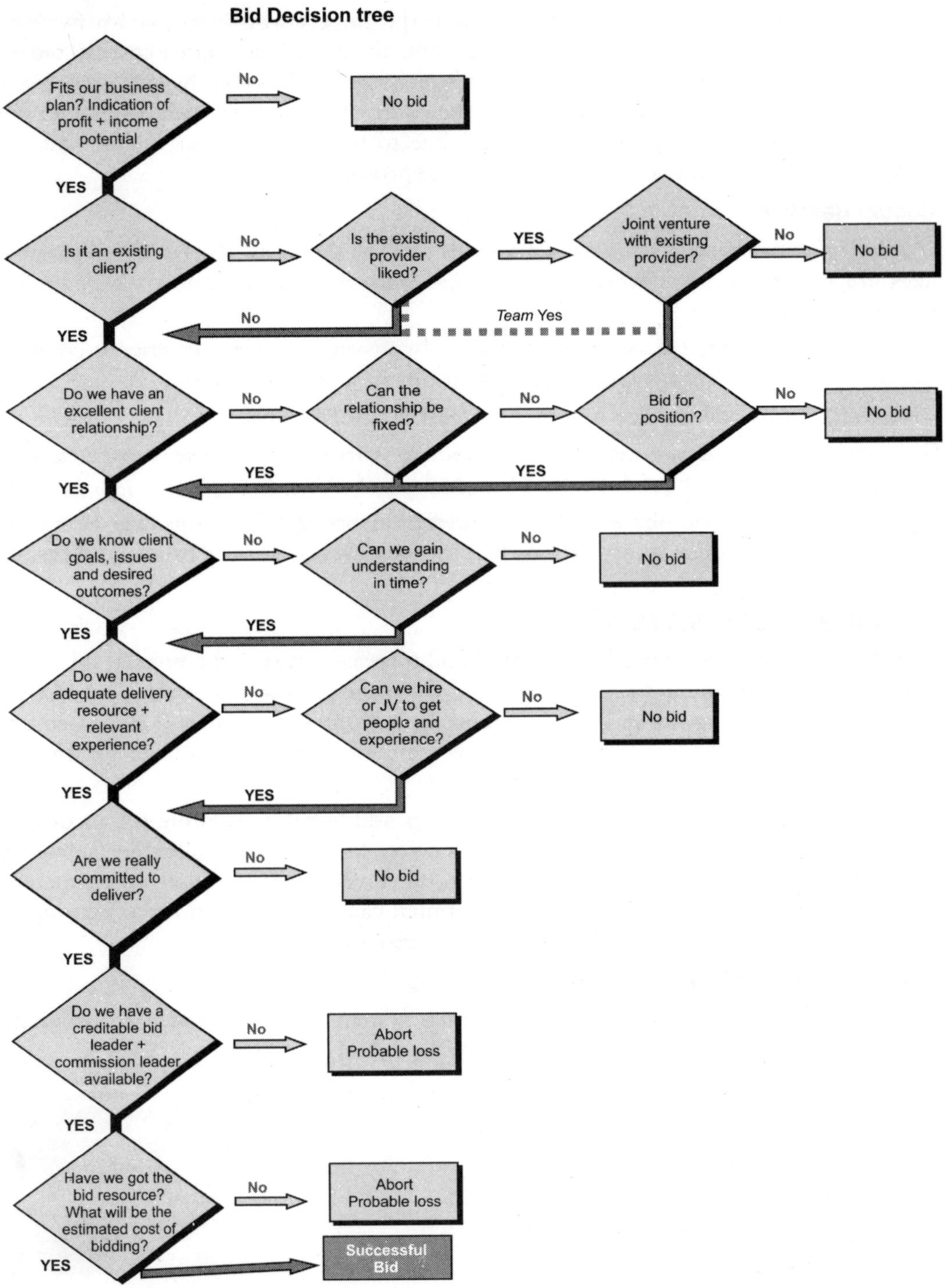

6.10 CONTRACT STATUS REPORT

Contract Status Report

Date:

WBS	
Project Manager	
Description	
Contract	
Contractor	

Budget	
Original Budget	
Current Budget	
Proposed Budget	

Forecast		
A. Commitments		
Contract Value		
Provisional Sum		
Contingency		
Dayworks		
Sub-Total		
Effective Contract Value		
Approved Variations		
Revised Contract Value		
B. Potential Commitments		
Pending Variations		
Pending Claims		
Others:		
ERIs		
DIs		
SIs		
Potential Claims		
Risks/Issues		
Provisional Sums		
Sub-Total (Others)		
Estimate (Future Works)		
Sub-Total (Pot. Commitments)		
Anticipated Final Cost (A + B)		
Variance (AFC - Current Budget)		

Contract	
Contract Start Date	
Contract Completion Date	
Contract Duration	
Defects Liability Expiry	
Works	
Forecast Start Date	
Forecast Completion Date	
Actual Start Date	
Actual Completion Date	
Revised Duration	
Forecast Complete	

Extension of Time	
Applied for by Contractor	
Assessed by Consultant/PM	
Approved by Owner/Client	
Revised Completion Date	

Payment Status	
Claimed	
Certified	
Retention	
L and A	
Net Certified	
Recovery of Advance Payment	
Actual Payment Due	
Actual Payment Received	

Advance Payment Bond	
Amount	
Ref. No.	
Bank	
Expiry Date	
Ext. Validity Date	

Advance Payment Bond	
Amount	
Ref. No.	
Bank	
Expiry Date	
Ext. Validity Date	

Insurance Expiry	
Contractors All Risks	
Third Party Liability	
Plant and Machinery	
Workmen's Comp	
Professional Indemnity	
Defects Liability	

Sample

6.11 DASHBOARD REPORT

PROJECT NAME: XX
PROJECT COST REPORT NO. 01

DASHBOARD

Detailed Cost Summary

Ref	Description	Controlled Cost Plan	Committed Costs	Un-committed Costs	Approved Variations	Anticipated Variations	Provisional Sum Adjustment	Value Engi-neering	Anticipated Final Cost
001	Main Contract	2,190,729	2,190,729	0	0	0	0	0	2,190,729
002	Professional Fees	0	0	0	0	0	0	0	0
Sub-Total		2,190,729	2,190,729	0	0	0	0	0	2,190,729
Construction Contingency		0	0	0	0	0	0	0	0
TOTAL COST		2,190,729	2,190,729	0	0	0	0	0	2,190,729

Cost Variance

	Variance + / (-)	Forecast Last Month + / (-)	Monthly Variance + / (-)
001 Main Contract	0	10,885,793	(8,695,064)
002 Professional Fees	0	640,600	(640,600)
Sub-Total	0	11,526,393	(9,335,664)
Construction Contingency	0	0	0
TOTAL COST	0	11,526,393	(9,335,664)

Employer's Representatives Instruction Status

Ageing Analysis

	Qty	Value	Qty Agreed	Value Agreed
< 30 Days	0	0	0	0
30 - 60 Days	0	0	0	0
60 - 90 Days	0	0	0	0
90 Days +	0	0	0	
Sub Total	0	0	0	0

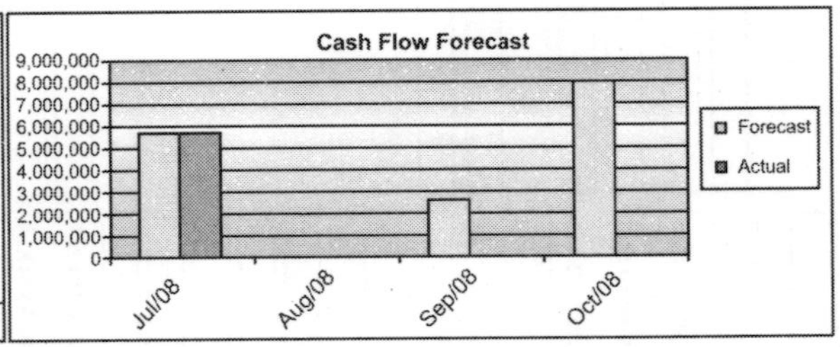

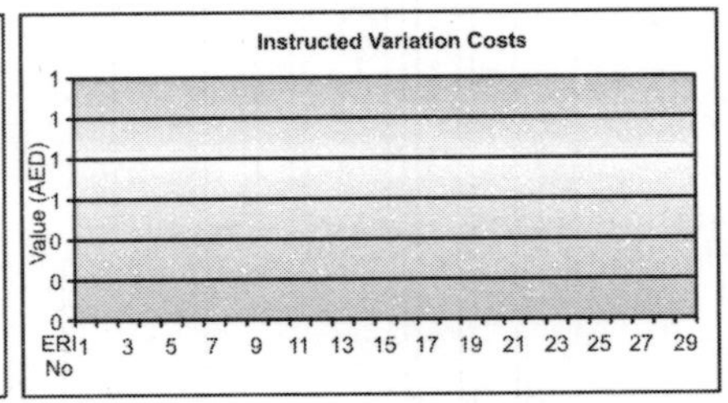

Alarm Bell

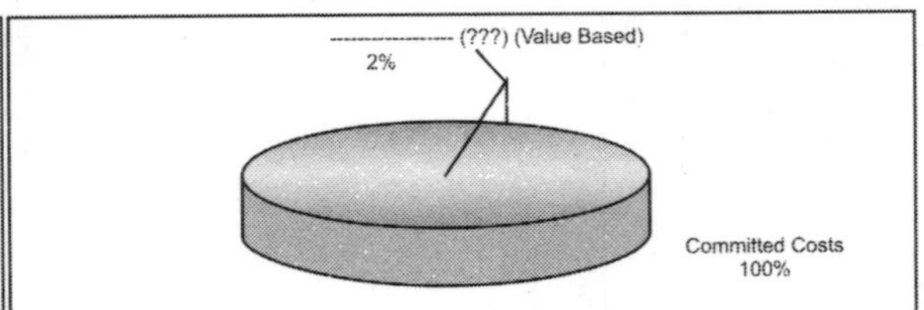

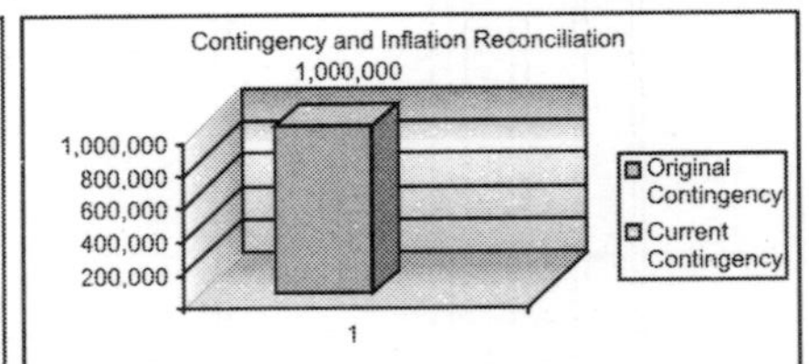

Case Flow Forecast

Month	Jul-08	Aug-08	Sep-08	Oct-08
Forecast	5,702,838		2,281,264	4,942,417
Actual	5,702,838			

6.12 CASH FLOW CURVE

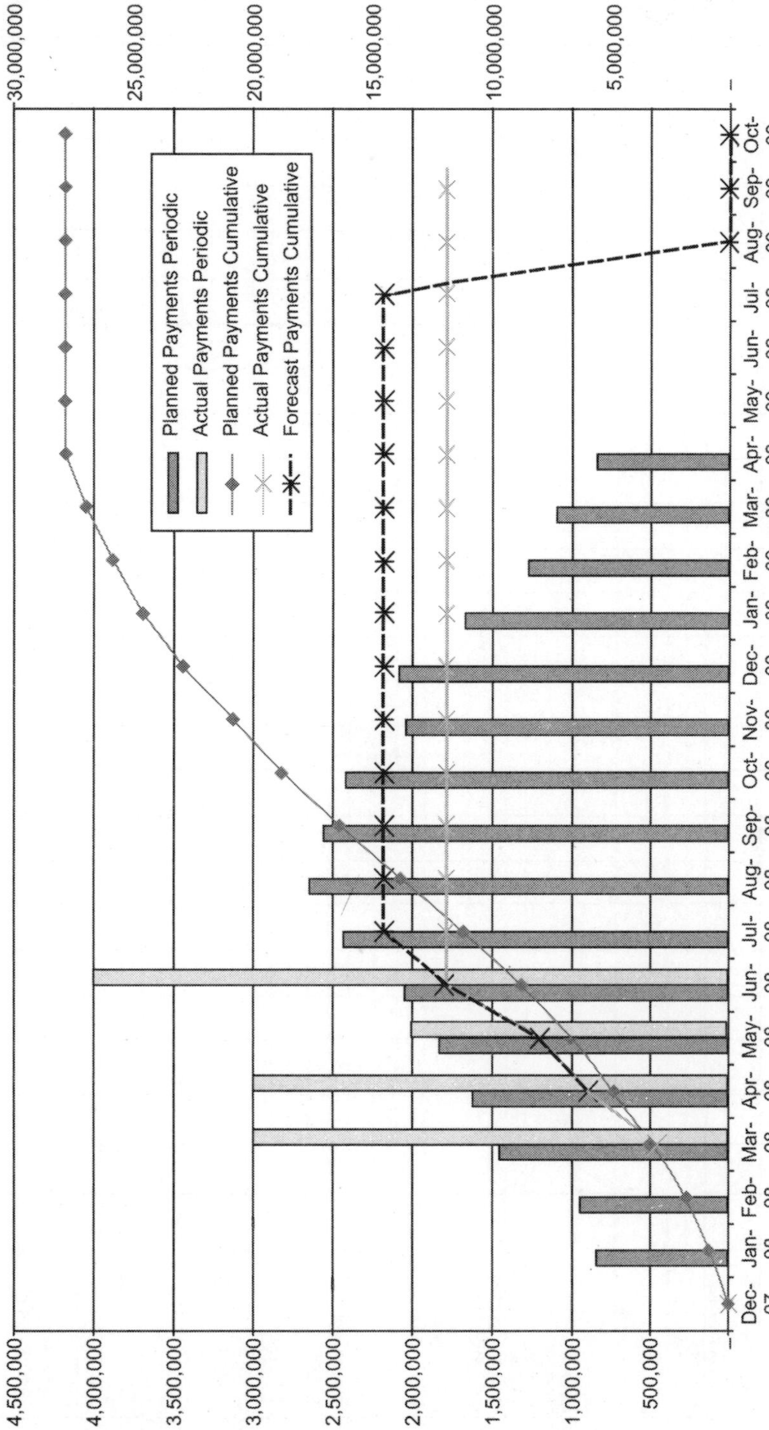

6.13 COST/CASH FLOW TABLE

COST/CASH FLOW

Sl No	Item	Projected Forecast Cost	Spent to date (Note 5)	Balance	Payment Due →	Apr-06	May-06	Jun-06	Jul-06	Aug-06	Sep-06	Oct-06	Nov-06	Dec-06	Jan-07	Feb-07	Mar-07	Apr-07	May-07	Jun-07	Jul-07	Aug-07	Sep-07	Oct-07	Nov-07	Dec-07	Jan-08		Jan-09
					Work Planned for →	*Mar-06*	*Apr-06*	*May-06*	*Jun-06*	*Jul-06*	*Aug-06*	*Sep-06*	*Oct-06*	*Nov-06*	*Dec-06*	*Jan-07*	*Feb-07*	*Mar-07*	*Apr-07*	*May-07*	*Jun-07*	*Jul-07*	*Aug-07*	*Sep-07*	*Oct-07*	*Nov-07*	*Dec-07*		
1	Excavation/Shoring/ Dewatering Works																												
2	DEWA Pipe Relocation																												
3	Main Contract																												
	Release of Retention																												
	Sub Total							ADVANCE for Main Contractor															Release of Retention-5%						
	Recommended Adjustment Budget																									Release of Retention-5%			
4	Excavation/Shoring/ Dewatering Works																												
5	Addn. Provisional sums/ Kitchen Equip./Home Theater sys																												
6	Contingency 10% (Item 1&2)																												
7	Inflation 8% (Item 1&2)																												
	Total Construction Cost																												
	Others—Consultant Fee/ Authority Fee, etc.																												
8	Design and Site Supervision																												
9	Quantity Survey																												
10	Quantity Survey																												
11	Structural Auditor																												
12	MEP Auditor																												
13	Elevator Consultant																												
14	Interior Designer																												
15	Building permit																												
16	Concept Design																												
17	Service Connection Charges																												
18	Soil Investigation																												
19	Soil Investigation																												
20	Advocate																												
21	Fencing																												
22	Signage																												
23	Digital Camera																												
24	Model																												
	Total Soft Cost	-	-	-																									
	GRAND TOTAL/MONTH	-	-	-		-	-	-	-	-	-	-	-	-	-	-	-	-	-	-	-	-	-	-	-	-	-	#	-
	Cumulative					-	-	-	-	-	-	-	-	-	-	-	-	-	-	-	-	-	-	-	-	-	-	#	-

Notes :
1. Not included Soft cost of Project Administration
2. Revised budget based on considering the awarded contracts
3. 10% Contingency on Enabling and Main Contract works
4. 8% Inflation on Enabling and Main Contract works
5. Spent to date value based on the information provided by Finance
6. Current Estimated Budget to be revisited pending new analysis from QS
7. All values in AED Millions

Sample

6.14 ANTICIPATED COST REPORT

Anticipated Final Cost Report (AFCR)

		Target Budget					Commitments					Potential Commitments						AFC	
		1	2	3	4	5	6	7	8	9	10	11	12	13	14	15	16	17	18
				= 1 + 2		= 3 + 4			= 6 + 7		= 8 + 9						= 11 + 12 + 13 + 14 + 15	= 10 + 16	= 17 – 3
WBS	Description	Original Budget	Approved Changes	Current Budget	Proposed Changes	Proposed Budget	Contract Value	Provi-sional Sums	Effective Contract Value	Approved Variations	Revised Contract Value	Pending Variations	Pending ERI's	Pending Claims	Future Works	Others	Total	AFC	Variance
				0		0			0		0						0	0	0
				0		0			0		0						0	0	0
				0		0			0		0						0	0	0
				0		0			0		0						0	0	0
				0		0			0		0						0	0	0
				0		0			0		0						0	0	0
				0		0			0		0						0	0	0
				0		0			0		0						0	0	0
				0		0			0		0						0	0	0
				0		0			0		0						0	0	0
				0		0			0		0						0	0	0
				0		0			0		0						0	0	0
				0		0			0		0						0	0	0
				0		0			0		0						0	0	0
				0		0			0		0						0	0	0
				0		0			0		0						0	0	0
				0		0			0		0						0	0	0
				0		0			0		0						0	0	0
				0		0			0		0						0	0	0
				0		0			0		0						0	0	0
	TOTALS	0	0	0	0	0	0	0	0	0	0	0		0	0	0	0	0	0

Sample Page 1

KEY:

No. 15 - Others - can be:
- Design Instructions
- Site Instructions
- Potential Claims
- Potential Miscellaneous Costs
- Etc.

AFCR - can be arranged by:
- Project
- Major Area
- Sub-Major Area
- Sama Dubai "V" Numbers
- Contracts (Consultants, Contractors, Etc.)

Supporting Detail Listings

e.g. Approved Changes, Proposed Changes, Approved Variations
Pending Variations, Pending Claims, etc.
- See Form 10 Listings

6.15 BUDGET TYPE VERSUS PROJECT STAGE TRACKING FORM

BUDGET TYPE VERSUS PROJECT STAGE TRACKING FORM

Box 1

Project Name ____________________ Job ref. # ______

Project Manager ____________________ Sponsor ______

- Concept Stage-Order of Magnitude Budget — File ref. # ______

Checked by/date ______ Signed-off by/date ______

- Schematic Design Stage—Study Budget — File ref. # ______

Checked by/date ______ Signed-off by/date ______

Comments on budget at the end of Schematic Design Stage gate

Box 2

- Detail Design Stage—Approval Budget — File ref. # ______

Checked by/date ______ Signed-off by/date ______

- Tender Stage—Tender Budget — File ref. # ______

Checked by/date ______ Signed-off by/date ______

Comments on budget at the end of Tender Stage gate

Box 3

- Construction Stage—Definitive Budget — File ref. # ______

Checked by/date ______ Signed-off by/date ______

Concluding comments on project budget including update periods, etc.

Sample Page 1

6.16 COST MANAGEMENT PLAN

COST MANAGEMENT PLAN

Box 1

Project Name ______________________ Job Ref. # [ ]

Project Manager ______________________ Sponsor ______________________

- Input Documents to the Cost Management Plan

Documents	Availability Yes	Availability No	Explain
• WBS	☐	☐	________
• OBS	☐	☐	________
• Project Time Schedule	☐	☐	________
________	☐	☐	________
________	☐	☐	________

Other Comments

Signed ______________________ (Project Manager) Date ________

Box 2

- Cost Budget approach to be used by stakeholders on their work package

☐ Performing Organization [ ]

☐ Service Provider(s) [ ]

☐ Specialist [ ]

☐ Contractor [ ]

Other Comments

- Estimating methodologies to be used

☐ Rates, etc. from a similar recent project Project name/ref [ ]

☐ Proprietary and published information Publications [ ]

☐ Bottom-up estimating

- Cost estimating method of resources and rates attached ☐ Yes ☐ No

Comments

- Methods to be used in measuring variances, controlling costs, forecasting, etc.

Document Attached ☐ Yes ☐ No *Comments*

Signed (Project Manager) Date ________

Sample Page 1

Value Engineering

7

Value Engineering is a formal and organized process to seek out the optimum value for the initial investment level and long-term cost.

7.1 OBJECTIVES OF VALUE ENGINEERING

- Have all the best solutions from all available options been designed into the project?
- Can the function and quality of a project be delivered at a reduced cost?
- Can improved function and quality be obtained at the same cost or lower?
- Can improved function and quality be obtained at a higher cost, but have benefits outweighing this cost?
- Can improved function and quality be obtained at a reduced cost, staying within acceptable limits of quality?

7.2 STRATEGY

The strategy that can be followed for Value Engineering is:

(a) Evaluating alternative material for construction (Imported versus Local) to ensure the lowest possible cost for material to meet the specification requirements; and

(b) Selection of the building systems and equipment that will optimize the initial investment and the life cycle cost.

Areas of Concern: Major areas of concern are that inappropriate materials and/or systems may be selected that are not in keeping with local conditions, or have high life cycle costs but low initial investments.

7.3 VALUE MANAGEMENT

Value Management (VM) is to be applied both formally and informally during development of the Project, regardless of capital cost. Formal VM Workshops will be held at key stages of the Project, regardless of capital cost.

Formal VM Workshops should be held at key stages of the project design effort under the guidance of a Value Manager. The frequency and stage at which they will be held depends on the type, size and complexity of the project and will be decided by the Project Manager together with the Value Manager. Usually, at least, one formal VM workshop is required very shortly after appointment.

The application of VM principles requires that all designers (including any design being developed by the trade contractors), adopt a challenging and systematic approach to their day-to-day work, and consider a full range of alternatives before a commitment is made to a specific solution. Contractors should be made aware of these requirements during the bidding process. It is imperative that VM principles are applied continuously throughout the design development. Only by considering performance criteria can value for money be achieved.

7.4 CONSTRUCTABILITY

An analysis of a project's Constructability includes review of the design with the focus on actual construction methods and materials. As such, it is a key component of the project Value Management effort. When carrying out assessment, reliance should be made to the company's extensive Site Management expertise gained from previous projects.

The assessment should take into account:

- Sequence
- Schedule (program)
- The chosen packaging of the elements
- Ease of construction and integration with other trades
- Delivery
- Achieving and specifying quality
- Preceding operations
- Subsequent works and risk of damage
- Risk of failures and defects
- Relevant hold points for inspections
- Ease of manufacture
- Ease of installation
- Safety
- Experience of the techniques employed
- Use of tried and tested technology
- Availability of materials and skills
- Maintainability

A close contact must be maintained throughout the detailed design development phase between the designers, the Project Manager and the Client team and the Value Manager to ensure that VM is being properly undertaken.

The designers must be committed to designing within the Cost Plan. Whilst every design decision should be subject to the VM process, the effort should be focused on the design elements which have the major impact on cost or on other important Client issues. It is known that, 80 per cent of the cost is contained within 20 per cent of the elements.

7.5 RESPONSIBILITY

The Project Manager with the Value Manager and the team, shall identify appropriate milestones during the design development phase and put it in place formalized, structures Value Management reviews of the brief and evolving design to ensure both continual compliance with the brief and value for money. The Task Groups can include any mix of project participants. They will carry out the following as an integral part of the design progress during design workshops:

- Carry out further brainstorming
- Develop ideas
- Carry out preliminary evaluation
- Submit options for further evaluation

Options will be evaluated against the following criteria:

- Operational effectiveness
- Flexibility/expandability
- User comfort
- Resources
- Capital cost effectiveness
- Operations and Maintenance (use of resource)
- Schedule (Program)
- Summarize recommendation

The valuation portions of the meetings are usually facilitated by a Value Manager.

7.6 TARGET WORKSHOP

When there is a need to probe further into specific elements of the project, if specific problems are encountered during the project delivery, or if changes are envisioned, a short value workshop can be undertaken to assess the best options and/or develop alternatives.

These workshops should be targeted and the team will consist of only those persons involved in the control process, with possible external consultants.

7.7 VALUE ENGINEERING PROGRAM

In an effort to eliminate the objections of a traditional program, the following criteria were developed for the program, and all parties—Owner, Architect/Engineer, and Professional Project Manager—are enlisted in carrying it out:

(a) The Project Manager, Owner, and Design Consultant will educate all their personnel to be on the lookout for alternate methods and concepts at any stage of the project. Suggestions are actively encouraged, and they are to be submitted to the manager.

(b) The Project Manager is given the responsibility for documenting and investigating initial feasibility and for preparing estimates and working out a presentation for all suggestions deemed feasible.

(c) The Design Consultant is given the responsibility for ruling on the engineering suitability of the suggestions and for making the determination as to whether the proposed suggestions is equal, superior, or inferior to the original concept.

(d) Together with an analysis of effects on the schedule or other like factors, all suggestions which are deemed technically feasible by the Design Consultant and which result in cost savings are submitted to the owner for final approval. In the event that significant redesign is required, the Owner will compensate the design consultant accordingly, and the design costs will be subtracted from the indicated savings.

(e) If possible, each bid package should contain several alternates that are equally acceptable to the Owner and Designer. Thus, the bidders themselves will participate in the program, and the owner will receive the benefit of bidder preference and current cost estimates.

(f) Potential bidders should be encouraged to develop alternates, which, if technically equal to the base bid, will receive consideration in evaluating bids. Thus, by its ingenuity, a bidder who is not low under the base bid may become the low bidder. The Owner receives a cost saving, and the ingenious bidder receives the contract.

(g) The criterion for determining whether a suggestion should be classified as a value-engineering savings is whether or not the saving is a result of the three-party team concept. (Suggestions may be made by any party—Owner, Manager, Designer, or event the construction contractors themselves.) If, in the final judgment of the Owner, it is a product of the three-party team, it is classified as a value-engineering saving and is documented by the Project Manager.

"There's never enough time to do it right the first time, but there is always enough time to do it over if it's wrong."

—R. Max Widerman (Fellow, Project Management Institute)

7.8 VALUE ENGINEERING RECOMMENDATION TEMPLATE

VALUE ENGINEERING RECOMMENDATION

Project : ____________________

Discipline : ____________________

VER # : ____________

Proposed By : ____________

Date Submitted : ____________

Page : 1 of ____

Current Estimate: : ____________

(Capex)

Baseline (Current Design): ____________ Brief description of the item as currently designed

(attached sketch, if reqd.) ____________

Proposed Alternative / Idea: ____________ Brief description of the proposed solution

(attach sketch, if reqd.) ____________

DISCUSSION

Advantages: ------------------------------

Describe Pros and Cons of accepting the proposed Idea/solution. Use additional sheets if necessary.

Disadvantages: ------------------------------

Impact on other units/disciplines/Schedule, etc..

Cost and time impact if implemented:

	Potential Cost or Time Savings (+) / Additional Cost or Time (–)						Status (A/R)
	SCHEDULE SAVINGS		COST SAVINGS (EXTRA)			Overall	
				Operating			
	No. of Weeks	Equivalent $ 'One Time' (1)	Capital Cost $	$/Year	NPV Equivalent (2)	Equivalent $ Present Value	
OPTION 1							
OPTION 2							
Weighted Criteria—Evaluation Score							

(1) 'One Time' schedule savings valued at $....k/week; (2) may be calculated outside the workshop, if necessary

RECOMMENDATIONS:

Action required ------------------------------

Action by (Name) ------------------------------

Completion Reqd. (date) ------------------------------

7.9 INFORMATION PHASE

INFORMATION PHASE

Project:

Location:

NOTE: Record important points when information is being presented during Workshop Phase 1.

PRESENTED INFORMATION Description	Presented By
Project overview by Client	
Project Constrains	
Important Issues	
Decision Criteria	
Process Overview	
Piping and Mechanical Overview	
Electrical and Process Controls	
Civil / Structural Overview	
Contracting and Procurement Strategy	
Life Cycle Costing Criteria (life of facility, interest rate, escalation rate, payback criteria, etc.)	

Page 1

7.10 VALUE ENGINEERING SUMMARY

VE RECOMMENDATION SUMMARY (VERS)

Project: *#REF* ______________________ *Date:* ______________

Location: ______________________

Group	Idea No.	Description	Risk High/ Med/Low	Potential Savings	Accept, Park, Reject (A, P, R)	Action Reqd./ Observations	Responsible Person(s)	Target Date
		Group 1						

Change Management

8

8.1 INTRODUCTION

Change orders (often interchangeably called 'Variations') document changes from the original scope of the contract, confirm schedule revisions, and set forth other modifications; they are issued, whether or not the amount of compensation to be paid to the Contractor will be affected.

The change order is generally written on a standard form and includes a complete but concise description of the change and its effect upon the contract schedule and price. Change order requests are normally reviewed by the PM Team/Owner's representative, who normally compares them with his own cost estimate of the change.

After his review and after negotiation with the Contractor if required, the representative may recommend acceptance by the owner, who in turn will formally approve and execute the change order.

Few construction contracts are completed without change. Changes or causes for change may be initiated by the designer, owner, regulatory agencies, others and the Contractor. Changed conditions occur when the actual physical or other jobsite conditions prove different from those foreseeable from the plans and specifications. Most minor changes are resolved on the job between the owner's representative and the Contractor. A change order is then added to the contract by mutual agreement.

Constructive changes result from the failure of the owner or his representative to recognize contractual entitlement to a change order or other changed condition in a timely manner. This type of disputed change is among the most difficult to adjudicate. A claim occurs when the parties cannot reach a mutually agreeable solution leading to a change order. Litigation, arbitration or alternate dispute resolution processes conducted by third parties are then usually employed.

But even when all parties to a contract are doing their level best to interpret its terms and conditions honestly and objectively, there are bound to be differences of opinion simply because of the specific interests of those involved in trying to get the job done as economically, quickly, and skilfully as possible.

Thus, there has evolved a body of law and accepted practices which help to achieve just, equitable, resolution of disputes. In contract, these often take the form of clauses pertaining to changed conditions, change orders, delays, contract time, liquidated damages, disputes, and claims.

Events Giving Rise to Changes, Claims and Disputes

Owner or Designer Changes (Owner or Designer Initiated)

- Numerous last-minute addenda during bid period
- Delay in access to the site
- Delay in furnishing approved for construction design drawings or clarifications
- Delay in furnishing owner-furnished items
- Defects in plans or specifications including errors and omissions
- Major design changes
- Many minor design changes
- Scope additions
- Scope deletions
- Schedule improvement directives
- Acceleration directives
- Suspension of work
- Interference by owner or his designated representative
- Non-performance by owner
- Termination of contract
- Equivocal or conflicting contract clauses
- Slow or inadequate response to submittals and requests for information

Contractor Changes (Contractor Initiated)

- Failure to start work as planned failure to supply a sufficient workforce
- Contractor performance failure
- Sub-contractor performance failure
- Supplier performance failure
- Installation of defective work
- Poor workmanship
- Schedule delay
- Sub-contractor schedule delay

Changes Caused by Others

- Unforeseen changed physical site underground or other conditions
- Other unforeseen site conditions
- Unusual weather or other natural event
- Regulatory agency change
- Change in the law
- Labour disputes

- Third-party interference
- Third-party non-performance

8.2 DOCUMENT INFORMATION SYSTEMS

Clearly, a system of information retention must be established that makes information easily retrievable for use toward resolving the issues.

The section herein discussing correspondence control presents document filing systems that keeps each document in an orderly manner.

However, accumulation of information to support issue resolution requires additional steps. Documents held in historical files must be retrieved from their sequential file and accumulated to a file for the specific issue.

The most convenient manual file search method involves the employment of document logs.

Document logs are maintained for all sequentially serial numbered documents including letters, requests for information, submittals, drawings, instructions, daily reports, minutes of meetings, and other project documents.

The descriptions of these items in the logs must provide sufficient information to determine whether any document concerns the issue at hand.

Information in any log must include the following minimal data:

- Sequential serial number
- Date of the document
- Name of issuer
- Name of recipient
- Concise summary description of contents
- Whether response is required
- Date response required
- Date of response
- Reference number of response
- Specification or drawing reference number (if applicable)
- Schedule activity number (if applicable)

Upon identification of a potential issue, the source document (the first document alluding to an issue that may give rise to a change) must trigger the set-up of a sequentially numbered "Issue" file and corresponding entry into an "Issue" log.

The information from the source document is tracked back through the project history to determine possible related documents. For example, a Contractor may write a letter stating that the response to an RFI may cause the Contractor to incur additional costs and may result in delays to the works.

The next step is to gather a copy of the RFI in question. The RFI likely refers to a drawing or a specification or perhaps to a field condition. The drawing or specification is reviewed for information that may lead to a schedule activity, or to a submittal, or other project document.

The field condition issue should indicate the date discovered for which daily reports are available indicating where the Contractor was working and what resources were available, the weather conditions and other information.

Once the file search has been completed, the issue file is current. An inventory of the file should be prepared and maintained at the front of the file.

The Contractor should be notified of the issue number and any subsequent correspondence of meeting discussions should refer to this issue number until resolution or final disposition is achieved.

Some issues may simply become inactive. The files are maintained and the identifying issue serial number is retained whether the issue is dormant or whether the issue progresses to a change order or if agreement cannot be reached to claim, arbitration or litigation.

The issue log becomes the initial log that progresses to the other logs as the issue develops. Once it is agreed that a change order is warranted, the issues log notes that a proposed change order has been initiated and the event passes to the change order process as prescribed in the contract documents.

Unresolved issues progress to the claims logs and other treatments.

Dormant issues remain until completion of the works and contract close-out.

8.3 VARIANCE REQUEST FLOW CHART

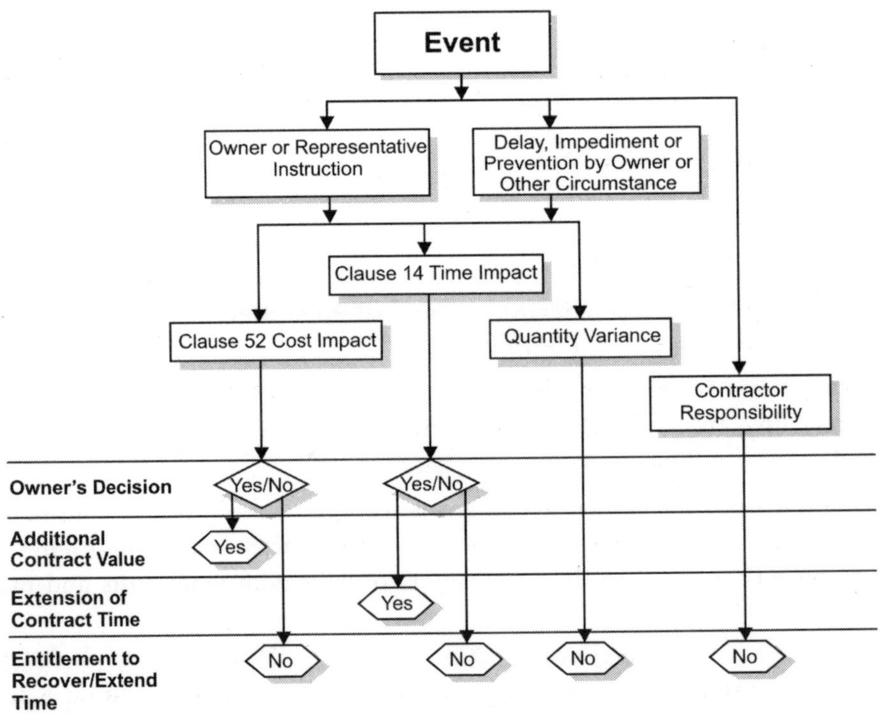

8.4 NOTICE OF VARIATION FORM

<table>
<tr><td colspan="2" align="center">[PROJECT NAME]</td></tr>
<tr><td align="center">Notice of Variation
Pursuant to Contract Clause(s)</td><td></td></tr>
<tr><td colspan="2">Notice of Variation From: Consultant ____ Contractor ____ NV# __________</td></tr>
<tr><td colspan="2">Details of Proposed Change:</td></tr>
<tr><td colspan="2">Related Documents:</td></tr>
<tr><td colspan="2">Justification: (Use attachments as necessary)</td></tr>
<tr><td colspan="2">Estimated Cost/Schedule Impact: (Use attachments as necessary)</td></tr>
<tr><td colspan="2">Submitted by:
Name: Signature: Designation:
Date:</td></tr>
</table>

8.5 VARIATION ORDER REGISTER

PROJECT NAME

Variation Order Register

28th February 2006

Sl. No.	Description (What)	VOR No.	Instigated By (Who)			Reason (Why)	Effects		CONSULTANT Action			COST CONSULTANT Action			PROJECT MANAGERS Action			CLIENT Comments			Change Order Agreed		Remarks
			Date	Ref:	Name		Cost	Program	Date	Ref.	Recommen-dation	Date	Ref.	Recommen-dation	Date	Ref.	Recommen-dation	Date	Ref.	(Yes/No)	Cost (AED)	Program	
TOTAL																							

Progress Measurement

9

9.1 INTRODUCTION

Having prepared the project schedule, the progress of the project must be measured, both in terms of physical work completed and time taken to complete. Many projects fail to deliver on time or in budget due to only measuring progress in the terms of work completed e.g. quantity installed or equipment erected then displayed on an "S" curve. This curve will not indicate where the project is in terms of time. A progress report is a combination of installed progress by quantity and a graphical display of the project activities by time. Using all the available reports and statistics, management can compare what was completed against what was planned, and take corrective actions if required.

9.2 METHODS OF PROGRESS MEASUREMENT

There are several methods for measuring progress, which should be determined and agreed at the start of the project. They are:

- Units completed
- Incremental milestones
- The start/finish method
- Supervisor opinion
- Weighted or Equivalent units

Units Completed—This is used for tasks that involve repeat production of easily measured items of work, when each item requires approximately the same effort of work.

Incremental Milestones—This is used where a pre-determined number of sub-tasks has been established and considered to be a milestone, and an agreed percentage allocated.

An example is pouring concrete:

Excavation and Lean Concrete—20%

Formwork—12%

Rebar and Embeds—15%

Pouring and Moisture Protection—25%

Stripping and Surface Preparation—15%

Shim Plates and Grout—5%

Backfill and Compaction—8%

The Start/Finish Method—An agreed percentage is assigned to the start of the task and given 100 per cent when the task is completed.

An example would be motor alignment. It could take hours or a few days; progress would be difficult to measure, therefore 50 per cent would be credited at the start of the task, and on completion, 100 per cent would claimed.

Supervisor Opinion—The Supervisor simply makes a judgment of the per cent complete of a specific task. Examples would be temporary works.

Weighted or Equivalent Units—This is used for tasks where the duration is long and they involve several sub-tasks.

An example would be structural steel erection, where:

Per cent complete = 83.5 ÷ 520.0 tons = 16.1%

Overall Project Progress—Main Weight Factors

The hierarchy for progress measurement shall be defined by the approved WBS. Home office services' progress measurements will include engineering, procurement, and contracts services. Material manufacturing and delivery progress will be based on manufacturing, fabrication and delivery milestones. Construction progress will be based on construction installed quantities.

The physical progress for the total project is obtained by summarizing the physical weighted progress of home office activities, material manufacturing and delivery and field activities according to the main weight factors of the Overall Project Progress.

Weight factors are based on cost value and/or man-hour budgets. Progress calculation will be performed at each contractual cut-off date.

Guidelines for Progress Measurement by Phase

General—Detail Engineering shall include all deliverables (drawings, specification, requisition, etc.), required to complete the work described in the Project Proposal and required to achieve Mechanical Completion. Most engineering Contractors have an in-house procedure for measuring progress, and as a rule, these systems are acceptable and it is not necessary or desirable to establish a separate system to meet the Client's requirements. When using a Contractor's system, the control emphasis should be on ensuring that all deliverables are included in the measuring system and that the planned dates support the intermediate and completion milestones in the project CPM schedule.

Engineering Measurement—The Contractor and the Client must identify the total number of deliverables included in the progress measurement system. Once the quantity has been established, then the steps in the development of each deliverable that will be used to determine progress must be determined. Following the establishment of the progress steps, weight must be assigned to each step. As stated above, most Contractors have a system established and the only effort in this phase is the determination of the number of deliverables, the effort for each class of deliverable, and the total man-hour budget.

The milestones are theoretical man-hours used to measure the progress during each stage of the document development. Therefore, based on the type of document to be issued e.g. P & ID's, loop diagram, etc. the milestones and weights assigned can vary.

The number of steps scheduled in the development of a deliverable can significantly vary. An example, with the % progress associated with each step is:

Step	Increment	Cumulative
Start draft	5%	5%
Issued for Review	45%	50%
Issued for Detailed Design	20%	70%
Final Issue	30%	100%

When the deliverables and progress measurement steps have been agreed to, the Contractor then must provide schedule dates for each step of each deliverable. This document becomes the plan. A copy of this approved original plan must be maintained to use as a baseline schedule.

Progress Calculations—As a rule, each step is either complete or not completed. There is no partial progress associated with a single step in the development of a deliverable. At the end of the report period, the total earned is tabulated. Progress is determined by the % of the total represented by the earned value. In most engineering systems, the earned % is compared to a progress "S" curve for the base plan, to determine if the project is on schedule. However, this progress represents physical progress and does not necessarily reflect schedule progress.

A separate analysis to determine if the steps completed were the steps scheduled must be made to determine schedule progress. Most systems for measuring engineering progress do not include a method of actually comparing planned vs. actual dates. To determine if the physical progress earned represents the scheduled progress, a manual comparison of the baseline plan to the updated plan must be made. Using the same weight, it is possible to determine the schedule status of the project. Procurement progress does not include the development of attachments to the documents e.g. technical evaluations, Calculating Procurement Progress and reporting Physical Per cent Complete.

Procurement Services—Progress shall be measured on a requisition basis, consistent with the WBS. Each requisition is weighted based on the estimated man-hours for that requisition relative to all other requisitions and subject to approval. Physical progress for each requisition shall be achieved based on standard milestones. The milestones used, progress milestones steps, and weight factors based on man-hour values are indicated below:

Issue Bidders List	5%
Issue RFQ to Bidders	10%
Complete Bid Tabs & Recommendations	15%
Issue Approved Purchase Order to Vendor	20%
Approved Shop Drawings Returned to Vendor	35%
First Inspection Certificates Issued	45%
First Equipment Ex-Works	50%
Final Equipment Ex-Works	70%
Final Inspection Certificates Issued	85%
Final Materials Delivery on Site	95%
Final Vendor Documentation Issued	100%

Equipment (including materials) manufacturing and delivery progress is measured by the detailed estimate or contract price. The dollar weight of each element shall be fixed, and progress shall be measured based on established milestones.

For Bulk Materials progress measurement, a budget quantity shall be initially established based on the detailed estimate or contract price of each order. Thereafter, the budgeted quantities shall be re-examined typically following successive design reviews to reflect current to-be installed quantities, and adjusted accordingly. Changes in the budgeted quantity for bulk material will impact the per cent completion calculation of that particular bulk, but shall not change the weighted contribution for that particular commodity unless an overall budget re-evaluation has been completed.

Construction Progress and Reporting Physical Per cent Complete—There are two types of progress: physical and schedule. Most contracts require the development of a Critical Path Method (CPM) schedule to establish the sequence and timing for the project execution and weighting of all construction activities to be used as a basis for progress payments.

Progress is normally represented as an "S" curve. The curve represents the plan for executing the project. Progress normally reported on the internal report is the actual physical progress, which is also used as the basis for incremental payments to the Contractor. Schedule progress requires additional analysis to determine if the physical progress achieved was also the work schedule.

Physical Progress Reporting—For purposes of payment, each activity is assigned a weight that should reflect the per cent of the overall effort represented by that activity. The method that is used to assign the weights should be reviewed and approved by all parties. As a general rule, the man-hour estimate is used to establish the weight of the elements such as electrical, piping, etc.

The weighted values are then distributed on the CPM scheduled activities. This distribution is used to generate an "S" curve that is used as the baseline progress schedule. Once the baseline "S" curve is established, the cumulative progress is compared to the baseline to determine if the project is on schedule.

The progress weighting should be reviewed to ensure that all activities are included and that the weightings are reasonable. The incremental (monthly) progress totals should be reviewed to ensure that the amount of progress in any given month is reasonable and represents the physical work schedule.

At the end of the report period, the Contractor submits a report of the completed activities. This report is verified and the weights of the completed activities are summed up. This value is the incremental progress for the report period. The progress is based solely on physical completion.

Incremental progress is added to the previous months' total to establish the cumulative progress. This is compared to the baseline "S" curve to determine if the physical progress is ahead or behind the planned value.

Since the physical progress does not consider when the work was scheduled, it is possible for a project to be physically ahead of schedule based on actual work accomplished but behind the CPM schedule when the work is evaluated to determine if the work being completed was actually scheduled.

Schedule Progress—A monthly update of the CPM schedule is required by most contracts. If a summary report is generated when the schedule is calculated in Primavera/other software, the indicated per cent complete is determined by the total number of work days completed divided by the total number of work days planned. This number does not take into account the resources assigned to activities and may not be a good indication of the schedule progress for the project.

If not performed by the Contractor and included in his monthly report, the following analysis should be performed monthly:

- Baseline schedule critical path progress vs. current schedule
- Current schedule critical path vs. baseline schedule
- Total float changes (for all paths)
- Activities scheduled to start for report period vs. activities actually started
- Activities scheduled to complete for the report period vs. activities actually completed
- A review of logic changes, including revised lags

"Is the project ahead of schedule and under spent?"

Risk Management

10

10.1 INTRODUCTION

All Projects face uncertainties throughout their development that can positively or negatively affect a project. Such uncertainties can be intrinsic or extrinsic to the project, such as political unrest or strikes. Be it a positive or negative outcome, all project uncertainties are broadly categorized as 'risks'. The identification, assessment and control of such risks are fundamental to the successful delivery of projects. Traditionally, risks may have been handled in an *ad hoc* manner, but increasingly, it is expected that risks be managed using a structured process.

Risk can be defined as the combination of the probability of an event and its consequences. In all types of undertaking, there is the potential for events to occur and resulting consequences that constitute opportunities for benefit or threat to success.

Risk Management is focused not just on the mechanics of handling risk but also on the broader strategic aspects, and is increasingly recognized as being concerned with both positive and negative aspects of risk.

Risk Management is a comprehensive and integrated approach that involves the identification, assessment and control/management of risks. The process is similar whatever the nature of the risks (e.g. safety, commercial, technical).

The objective of Risk Management is to add value to all the activities in the project by managing out the risks so the full implications are not felt. It combines the understanding of the potential upside and downside of all those factors which can affect a project. It increases the probability of success and decreases the probability of project failure.

Risk Management should be a continuous and developing process which runs throughout the project's duration and addresses the widest possible range of risks and uncertainties.

10.2 RISK MANAGEMENT CONCEPT

Risk Management is a continuous process, which starts with Project Definition and is applied to every subsequent assessment, decision and action. It is sometimes defined as the 'What if...?' approach.

At the Project Definition stage, there is strict adherence to the provisions of the Risk Management Manual and application of the Risk and Opportunity Management Policy. The resulting Risk Control Plan provides all stakeholders with a clear view of the risks involved in a project, and enables them to make appropriate adjustments, provisions and contingency plans.

As the project develops, while the Risk Control Plan governs management decisions, Risk Management must become part of every person's thought process-in everything they do. In practical terms, everyone must continually 'think safety', 'think cost' and 'think time'.

Key Procedural Roles and Responsibilities

This section provides details for the roles and responsibilities of key personnel in managing risk within the organization.

Project Manager

The Project Manager bears ultimate responsibility for identifying, reducing, managing and—wherever possible—eliminating risk within a project.

Manager, Engineer and Supervisor

Every manager, engineer and supervisor is responsible for identifying, reducing, managing and attempting to eliminate risk within their field of operations.

Individual Employee Organization Wide

Every individual throughout the Organization is responsible for his own safety, efficiency and security. This includes the work they are doing, the tools they are using and the people they are working with, including Client, Sub-contractor and Contractor personnel.

10.3 BENEFITS

- Projects will have a clear execution plan from day one, from the Supply Chain point of view.
- By introduction of accurate tracking and forecasting of the materials, the team and the Management can always know where the project stands and which areas of concern need immediate attention.
- Frequent periodic status reports would provide feedback to the Planning and Controls department, which in turn would help in reporting and rescheduling the remaining activities more accurately.
- By introducing and implementing effective materials procurement, control and inventory procedures, substantial cost savings can be envisaged.
- By following the Bid receipt and evaluation procedures, any risks of malpractices would be minimized.
- At project definition stage:
  - Promotes clarification of Business objectives
  - Aids clearer definition of the project
  - Produces a better understanding of factors affecting its successful delivery
  - Early application will uncover what the real risks are and provide more options to deal with them
  - Provides an objective view of the risks to the project (versus subjective)
- At the project implementation stage:
  - Aids selection and alignment of Project Team

- If applied well, it will assist in team building and bring greater trust, confidence and commitment
- Ensures ownership of and responsibilities for risks are clearly understood
- Promotes a 'can do' attitude in the Project Team
- Can unearth opportunities (ways of doing the project quicker, cheaper, better)
- Leads to greater confidence in project outturn
- Supports other Project Management tools and techniques
- Provides a method and vehicle for proactive Client involvement
- Allows specific risks to be managed by the party best equipped to deal with them, at least cost.

The maximum benefit of RM will be gained by applying it at the commencement of the project life cycle, when there will be more options available to control the risks and the decisions taken will have the greatest influence. However, the process is one of diminishing returns; a judgment needs to be made on how much time and effort to devote to the process. Maximum benefit will be derived from identifying 'show stopping' risks and formulating a plan to deal with them, rather than addressing every conceivable risk. Consequently, in order to realise this benefit, it is essential to have Client and key Project Team members involved in, and committed to, the process.

RM is not an exact science and will not identify all risks; it has to be accepted that the process will deliver returns in proportion to the quality of thought and effort put in.

Whilst RM is concentrated on risks that may have an adverse affect on the outcome of the project, it is also capable of identifying positive opportunities. Whether or not this feature is incorporated into the process, the Project Manager should communicate to the Project Team the requirements and objectives of RM.

10.4 ASSOCIATED RISKS OF NOT FOLLOWING PROCEDURES

The consequences of a risk ignored can be devastating to a project, with critical implications for the Client, Stakeholder's reputation, profitability and individuals' health and well-being. Therefore, whether it's a poor procurement decision (which may lead to using sub-standard materials, failed inspections, missed deadlines or overpayment to suppliers)—or unguarded machinery (lost-time accidents, injury, death and financial penalties), it is essential that all risks be effectively managed—with continuous forward thinking and prompt, accurate reporting by individuals at every level.

It is the Project Manager's responsibility to ensure, through appropriate training, communication and reporting systems, that all relevant time, cost, procurement, logistic and safety issues are subjected to an effective Risk Management Procedure. It is *everyone's* responsibility to be Risk-Aware and to manage/report perceived risks.

Flowchart for Project Risk Management

Action	Responsibility
Define the Project	
Establish Project Risk Management Requirements	Project Manager
Threat Identification (What are the risks?)	Stakeholders
Risk Assessment (How significant are they?)	Stakeholders
Risk Control Planning (What can we do? What will we do?)	Stakeholders
Risk Reporting (Do it and monitor outcome)	Risk Action Owners

10.5 RISK MANAGEMENT PROCESS

Application

The Project Manager, having participated in establishing the Project Risk Management Requirements, uses it as the basis of his Risk Control Plan. Managers, Engineers and Supervisors must be familiar with the Plan and adhere to the procedures defined within it.

Every individual involved in a project must be familiar with the basic elements of Risk Management:

- ***Eliminate*** perceived risks wherever possible.
- ***Transfer*** risk to the person or entity best placed or qualified to deal with it.
- ***Reduce*** the likelihood or impact of an event.
- ***Accept*** the inevitable—but make contingency/recovery plans.

All too often, Risk Management is viewed as just another 'tick the box' process, designed to impede constructive work. Nothing could be further from the truth: The paperwork involved is simply to record that the risks have been identified, addressed and managed.

The Risk Notice system and Risk Register must be designed to follow the Work Breakdown Structure as far as possible, so that Risk Management becomes an integral part of 'normal' management procedures. Failing that, Risk Management will be seen as an impediment to progress and become a chore.

Just as efficient procurement and time management are profit centre's for the project, Risk Management is an essential tool for maintaining the profit margins on which Stakeholder business depends. Individuals must be instructed to ask themselves, whenever an unplanned or unexpected event occurs or is foreseen, "How could this affect my pay, my job, and my health or Stakeholder's business?" If the answer is negative, a risk or threat has been identified. Supervisors must repeat this instruction at every opportunity—and record in their own journals that it has been done.

Once a project has started, formal Risk Management record systems are limited to recording, monitoring and reporting new, or previously undetected, risks. However, the process of thinking ahead, anticipating threats and identifying risks at every level is continuous. Individuals below the level of Supervisor must be encouraged to make oral reports to their supervisor, without fear of criticism or punishment. Supervisors will then convert those oral reports into a Risk Report.

Threat Identification

Threats to the project may materialize from many sources and are a result of uncertainties within a boundary constraint (e.g. performance specification, time deadline, sanctioned finance, etc.). However, some research suggests that 80 per cent of project risks are attributable to people involved in the process. This area is somewhat more difficult to quantify than others, but must not be ignored when implementing the Risk Management process.

There are a number of techniques that can be initiated within the 'normal' Project Team; there is also that requiring specialist assistance. In each case, the process at this stage should concentrate on the 'cause', although noting the potential 'effect' may subsequently help in the risk assessment.

- **Assumptions review**—a methodical trawl through all the assumptions made at an earlier project stage to test their validity and establish what threats would be posted if the assumption proved invalid.
- **Brainstorm**—typically, a Project Team meeting with the agenda 'what could go wrong'?
- **Interview**—typically, a one to one review by the Project Manager with Project Team Members, Client representatives, other stakeholders, etc.
- **Prompt list**—a generic list of prompts that may be used on a variety of projects.
- **Checklist**—usually, a list generated from past experience of similar projects.
- **Specialist techniques**—from a variety of disciplines, depending on the nature of unique or unusual aspects of the project.

Depending upon the scope/complexity of the project, it may be appropriate to employ a skilled facilitator on any of the above processes.

Whichever technique is used, an 'open' approach should be adopted—involving all stakeholders wherever possible. A record should be kept of all the threats identified, even if it is ultimately decided that they are sufficiently minor not to warrant further action. This is often helpful later on, should events change.

Threat Prompt/Checklist

The Threat Prompt/Checklist form contains a list of typical sources of project risk.

The user of the Form assumes that the Project Process is being used and that all the requirements and guidance therein is being applied. If not, additional risks may be present and will need to be addressed.

Research into the reasons for project failure has identified the following as the major causes:

- Getting the wrong project (e.g. the reasons for the project and its objectives not being sufficiently elaborated)
- The wrong environment (e.g. the business environment surrounding the project not being conducive to successful execution)
- People (inappropriate selection, inadequate skills, wrong attitude, different agendas)
- Ineffective execution (the project process and tools/techniques being inadequate)

The checklist therefore concentrates on these areas:

Risk Assessment

Following the identification of threats, it is necessary to validate and rank them in some way so that any subsequent control measures can be commensurate with the perceived level of risk.

This process requires two features to be assessed:

- The likelihood/probability of the threat occurring
- The impact/effect on the project should the threat materialise.

Further, the impact may be assessed in terms of effect on either:

- Cost
- Schedule
- Performance—for asset investment projects this may include product quality, production capacity, operating cost, plant availability and reliability, etc. or
- Safety Health Environment—this is often included as a sub-set of performance, above.

The magnitude of risk can be expressed as:

Risk-Likelihood × Impact

It is, therefore, common to identify Likelihood and Impacts as being High, Medium or Low and represent risks using a 3 × 3 matrix. By adopting a simple numbering system, it is relatively easy to rank risks:

	H	3	2	1
Likelihood	M	4	3	2
	L	5	4	3
		L	M	H
	Impact			

Using this system, it would be appropriate to address all the '1's first, followed by the others in numerical order. However, in order for the ranking system to be meaningful, the sensitivity of High, Medium and Low for both Likelihood and Impact and for the three (or four) impact effects needs to be considered; e.g. is a High Likelihood and Low Impact (3), the same magnitude of risk as a Medium Likelihood and Medium Impact (3)? This is often a difficult and somewhat subjective judgment. Theoretically, these parameters should be calibrated prior to ranking (see below), but in reality it is more important to make an assessment and prioritize the risks, than to ponder unduly over the numerical accuracy of the assessment.

Risk Calibration Examples

Scale	Likelihood	Impact on Project		
		Schedule	Cost	Performance
High	20-50%	>20%	>15%	Major shortfall in key parameters
Medium	5-20%	10-20%	5-15%	Minor shortfall in key parameters
Low	<5%	<10%	<5%	Some shortfall in secondary parameters

Note: Any threat with a likelihood of >50% is such a high level threat that it should be treated as something that will probably happen, with a risk that it will not.

More sophisticated techniques are available to give a quantitative assessment of risks. These often involve:

- Converting all impacts into costs, to aid prioritization.

  Note: Some research suggests that potential time and performance losses usually far outweigh potential cost losses.
- Assessing likelihood as probability values.
- The use of statistical techniques (Monte Carlo simulation) to establish measures of overall project risks.

Risk Control Planning

There is little value in identifying threats and assessing the risks if no attempt is made to plan to mitigate their potential adverse effects. The questions to be addressed at this stage are:

- What can we do?
- What will we do?

The basic choices available are:

- **Eliminate**—take action to remove the risk completely.
- **Transfer**—a recognition that the risk will still exist but it will be allocated to the party most able to deal with it (RM is more than cost) (e.g. Client, Contractor, etc.). In some cases, these risks may be transferred to an insurance company (e.g. for currency exchange). Transferring the risk will only be effective if the party carrying the risk is aware of it and has a plan to deal with it.
- **Reduce**—take action to lower either the likelihood or impact of an event happening.
- **Accept**—acknowledge that the risk exists but do nothing to prevent or reduce it.

For either Reduce or Accept, it may be necessary to produce a contingency/recovery plan, to be enacted if the risk materializes.

With all control measures, it is important to keep an equitable balance between the potential consequences of the risk and the measures taken to deal with it. Converting all risk impacts into cost and schedule equivalents helps to produce a clearer understanding of these decisions.

When determining the appropriate action to deal with each risk, it is important to allocate ownership of the resulting action (basic options are Project Team members, Client, Supplier and Contractor). It is desirable to have a single specified accountable "Risk Action Owner" for each action.

Each basic action agreed usually needs to be followed by a more detail plan of how the mitigation will be achieved. These plans need to be reviewed carefully with the Risk Action Owner and other affected parties, as very often, the control measures will produce secondary risks that were not evident in the first review. In some cases fallback plans will be necessary.

Risk Reporting

It is recommended that a Risk Notice system and a centralised Risk Register be used for recording, monitoring and reporting of risks. The way in which the risks are numbered needs to be determined to suit the project, although following the Work Breakdown Structure is a good basis.

The management of risks needs to be integrated into 'normal' management of the project; action will result in activities on the program and associated costs. These should be progressed and reported along with other activities, although it is suggested that a risk be included as separate reporting items in both the progress meetings and project reports.

The objective of reporting is to ensure regular review of the status of risks (Does the threat still exist? Is there any significant change in likelihood or impact?) and progress on the agreed actions; also to identify any additional threats. The latter becomes particularly relevant when there are changes from how the project was first planned.

Some risks may be so significant that they pose a threat to the viability of the whole project. The process for dealing with these is fundamentally the same, although they may require special reporting to the Client in order to elicit the appropriate business response.

Application of RM

The extent to which RM is implemented at work package level needs to be agreed between the Project Manager and the Work Package Owners. Each work package will have risks to its successful delivery; the more significant of these are usually progressed at a project level. However, the Work Package Owner is responsible for delivery of the Work Package within the agreed parameters, and should adopt the principles of RM given in this manual.

The method by, and extent to which RM is applied on a project needs to be established and recorded in the Project Execution Plan and taken into account in the baseline project estimate and schedule. This would normally include the initial risk assessment and agreed action. Those risks that subsequently materialize would normally be regarded as changes to the baseline schedule and be transferred to the project change control system.

Responsibilities

The Project Manager should:

- Consider, establish and communicate the extent to which RM is to be applied on a project.
- Ensure that appropriate people are involved and appropriate techniques are employed to identify threats, assess and prioritize the resulting risks, and determine appropriate actions.
- Record, review, revise and report risks using a Risk Register.
- Agree with Work Package Owners the extent to which RM is implemented at a Work Package Level.

Work Package Owners should implement RM at a work package level, to the extent agreed with the Project Manager.

"There's never enough time to do it right the first time, but there is always enough time to do it over if it's wrong."

—R. Max Wideman (Fellow, Project Management Institute)

10.6 RISK REGISTER SAMPLE

Risk/ Issue No.	Risk/Issue Raiser	Date Raised	Date last updated	Target Date for mitigation	Description and Impact	P	I	Automated Priority Rating (RAG)	Risk Owner	Actions / Progress to Date	Status (Open / Closed)	Date Closed

Probability	Impact: Low	Impact: Medium	Impact: High
Low	Green	Green	Amber
Medium	Green	Amber	Red
High	Amber	Red	Red

Communication Management

11

11.1 INTRODUCTION

The communication procedures define the requirements for communications between the Project team members and also provide the format for the various forms to be used on the Project Flow of communication is based on a need-to-know basis. Timely communications are essential for the successful execution of any Project. It is vital that the Employer be kept advised of all critical aspects of the Project on a current basis.

Language: The language to be used on all oral and written communications relating to the Project shall be English. Contracts shall be written in English.

Form of Communications: Communications shall include design and construction drawings, specifications, schedules, calculations, reports, letters, facsimiles, e-mails, transmittals, memoranda, meeting minutes as well as verbal instructions.

Reference Dating: All written correspondence shall have a specific reference code and replies shall refer this code. To avoid the confusion arising from the use of mm-dd-yy format by some parties and the use of dd-mm-yy by others, the standard format to be used on the Project shall be the Gregorian calendar using the day, month, and year format (either 06-Jan-04 or 06 January 2004) shall be used.

Project and Single Subject: All correspondence should indicate the Project name and deal with only one subject. The contents should clearly address the particular subject.

Oral Communication: All formal oral communication should be confirmed in writing as early as possible but no later than the period indicated in the relevant contracts/agreements.

Acknowledgment of Receipt: The receiver when specifically requested shall acknowledge receipt of correspondence in writing. In most cases, the recipient shall acknowledge receipt by signing the correspondence delivery log book of the originator or by signing and stamping as 'received' on a photocopy of the document.

11.2 STANDARD FORMS

To the extent possible, all correspondence shall be on standardized communication forms to allow for management of information flow.

Logs, defining originator, recipient, date of issue, date of response required, days outstanding, date response received, are to be established for all communication forms and these logs are to be maintained by the originator. The intent is to monitor the responsiveness of parties and to avoid or minimize tardy responses that impact the Project.

Specific logs are to be implemented for such items as:

- Request for Information
- Transmittals
- Contractor Submittals
- Approval Letters
- Requests for Variation Orders
- Project Manager's Instructions
- Consultant's Instructions
- Variation Orders

11.3 MEETINGS

Various types of meetings shall be conducted between Project Team Members. Formal meetings between Team Members are meetings specified in the work program of the Team Members including:

Executive Meetings: Meetings between the senior management personnel from the Employer, the Project Manager, the Design Consultant and the Quantity Surveyor shall be held as desired by the Employer.

Project Meetings: Meetings between the Employer, the Project Manager, the Quantity Surveyor, and the Design Consultant are Project meetings. These meetings shall be held on a weekly basis and chaired by the Project Manager.

Design Meetings: These meetings shall be held on a regular basis, primarily for the purpose of the presentation of design status by the Design Consultant and obtaining Employer approval of design progress documentation. The Design Consultant chairs the Design Meetings.

Contractors Progress Meetings: These meetings are held to review construction progress, status of submittals, information required, and critical issues. These meetings are chaired by the Project Manager and attended by the Design Consultant, the Supervision Consultant, the Quantity Surveyor and the respective Contractor. The frequency of these meetings shall be weekly.

Other Meetings: These are not held periodically, but for specific purposes are similar to: Meetings to review, presentation and approval of specified deliverables. Interim meetings to be held at regular intervals to review work progress.

Minutes of Meetings shall be prepared and distributed by the Team Member chairing the meeting. Copies of the minutes shall be distributed to all attendees as well as Employer and others as required for information. Comments on notes shall be submitted within three (3) days otherwise the notes shall be considered as accurate.

11.4 DOCUMENT FLOW AND CONTROL FORMS

Document Flow Matrix—Construction: This matrix should explain the routing of various documents, reports and control forms.

Engineers Instruction (for Technical matters): EI is a form to be used to issue instructions to the Contractors that are not meant to entail additional time or money. EIs are issued to the

Contractor by the Consultant for technical matters for clarifying the drawings, specifications, site conditions, quality, etc. as 'non-variation' instructions. EIs issued by the Consultant will require to be signed by the Project Manager.

Variation Order and Request for Variation Order: Requests for Variation Orders may be raised either by the Project Manager or by the Consultant for work that entails additional time and/or cost to the Contractor. The details of the work intended to be instructed as a Variation Order are described in the Request for Variation Order. The impact of time, if any, is estimated by the Project Manager and the impact of cost, if any, is estimated by the Quantity Surveyor. The Request for Variation Order is sent for approval of the Employer along with a duly completed Variation Order that is intended to be issued to the Contractor. Employer's approval of the Request for Variation Order is recorded by endorsing the Variation Order by signing and stamping by the Employer's authorized representative. The Employer's signed Variation Order is then issued by the Project Manager to the Contractor as an instruction to execute the said variation to his contract. A Variation Order is the essential authority for the contract sum or contract time schedule to be adjusted and allows the Contractor to get paid and is also the authority to the Contractor to change work, quantities, etc.

Payment Certificate (PC): Applications for payment are made by the Contractor and forwarded to the Project Manager for review and recommendation. The Project Manager shall, upon his review of the Contractor's work performed during the period for which the payment application is raised, forwards the Contractor's application for payment to the Quantity Surveyor. The Quantity Surveyor verifies the rates, prices and an amount claimed by the Contractor for payment and issues the Payment Certificate to the Employer to distribute payments.

Request for Information (RFI): The RFI is used by the Contractor to request technical information from the Consultant, who will respond on the same form. The RFI response shall be distributed to all other concerned parties who may be affected by the response or who will require for the coordination of work including other package contractors. All RFIs are assigned consecutive numbers for each contract. The turn around time for RFI shall be 7 working days maximum. However, cases where immediate attention of the Consultant/the Project Manager is required, attempts will be made to provide speedier response.

Transmittal Form: This form shall be used by the Contractor for the transmission of all technical submittals i.e., shop drawings, samples, guarantees, manufacturer's data, certificates, test reports, etc. and the Consultant shall respond on the same form. The submittal response shall be distributed to the Project Manager and any other party, which the response may affect or require for the coordination of work.

Submittal Sample Tag: This tag shall be used by the contractor for labelling all submittal samples.

Specification Comparison Sheet: This form shall be used by the Contractor for the comparison of contract requirements against any proposed alternate material or details.

Material Inspection Request (MIR): The Material Inspection form shall be prepared by the Contractor and submitted to the Consultant for his technical acceptance and verified by the

Project Manager for quantity. The Project Manager shall utilize this, upon verification, for contractor payment purposes.

Works Inspection Request (WIR): This form shall be completed and submitted by the contractor to the Consultant in advance providing adequate time for inspection.

Daily Report: A Daily Report is required from the Contractor using the form provided by the Project Manager. The report describes the Contractor's workforce and work activities on a daily basis. The Project Manager shall provide the Contractor with specific report requirements for major work activities as the work progresses. These daily reports shall commence from the date that the contractor commences his on-site activity.

Activities to Commence—One Week Look-ahead: This form for one week look-ahead for commencement of new works shall be filled-up to enable advance notification to the other contractors for coordination purposes.

Submittal Status Report (SSR): The SSR is updated on a weekly or bi-monthly basis by the Contractor on all his technical submittals. Included in this group of submittals are shop drawings, samples, guarantees, manufacturer's data, certificates, test reports, etc. The specific requirements of each submittal shall be as defined in the specifications.

Procurement Status Report (PSR): The PSR is updated on a weekly or bi-monthly basis by the Contractor detailing the status of all his material purchase, delivery, and installation schedules.

Status of Instructions/Information Requests (SI/IR): The SI/IR is updated on a weekly or bi-monthly basis by the contractor detailing the status of all PMI's, SCI's, VO's, RFI's, etc.

"The problem with communication…is the illusion that it has been accomplished."

—George Bernard Shaw

11.5 CORRESPONDENCE FLOW CHART

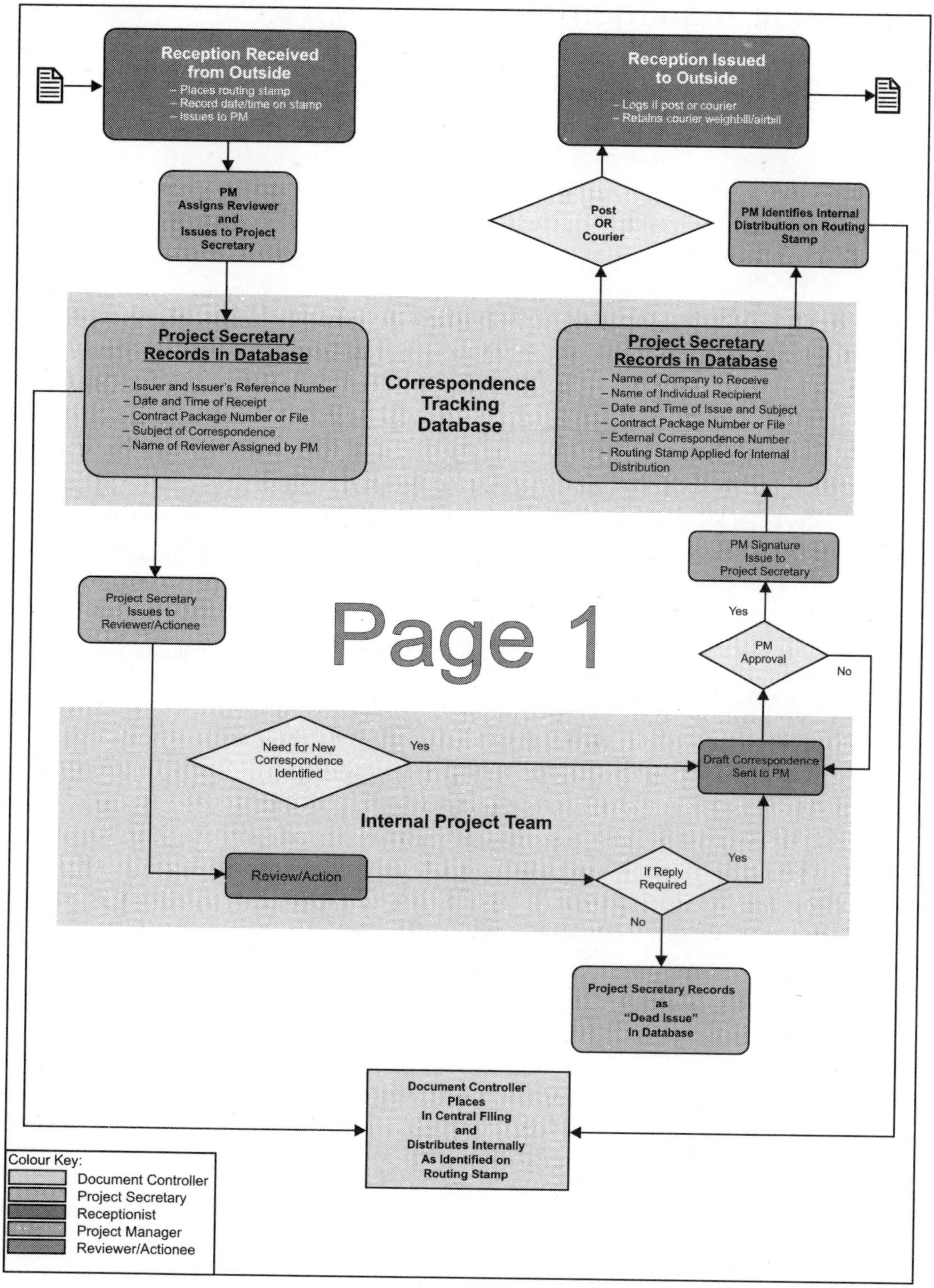

Earned Value Management

12

12.1 INTRODUCTION

According to the Project Management Body of Knowledge, Earn Value Analysis in its various forms is the most commonly used method of performance measurement. It integrates scope, cost (or resource), and schedule measures to help the Project management team assess project performance. Earn value analysis is consider as a three-dimensional tool—it compares the amount of work planned with the amount achieved, and compares this with the "cost" of that achievement. Performance is assessed mathematically and expressed in "Key Performance Indicators". The indices are then used to forecast final outcome—and past experience shows this forecast is likely to be accurate unless some changes are made. Earn Value Analysis reports are therefore a spur to action, focusing attention on the major problems. Also, by directing management attention to the most critical problems, focus can be placed on the critical areas of a project.

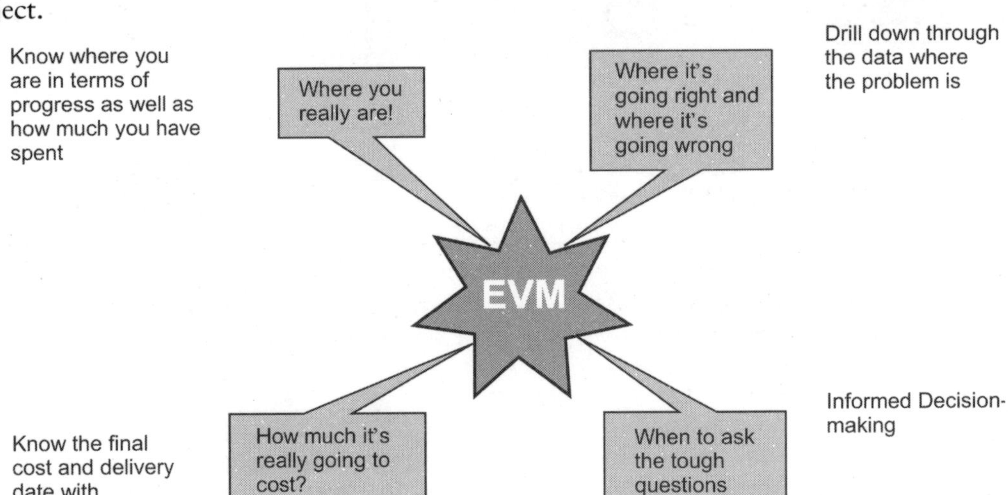

Earn Value Analysis preparation commences in the planning stage of the project. Estimated costs and resources are added to each activity defined in the program of works. Percentage completion of each activity is regularly assessed, usually weekly, and entered into the planning software which calculates planned and earned value data automatically. Actual labour used is imported from daily labour returns and actual costs to date from existing commercial systems. (For smaller projects, spreadsheets have been established which manage the whole process without reference to planning software.)

If all this sounds complicated, it is worth noting that for most projects, once the routine is established the production of Earn Value Analysis reports takes only a couple of hours or so a week-time that should be spent producing some sort of progress report anyway. Earn value Analysis gives the Project Manager the tools to consider the position of the project accurately and what remedial measures are necessary to recover any lost time.

12.2 ADVANTAGES OF EARN VALUE ANALYSIS

Better Visibility into Program Performance

Earned value analysis yields earlier and better visibility into program performance than is provided by non-integrated method of planning and control as every activity is weighted at the outset and regularly measured. When the plan has been developed to a level of detail where activities have duration of say two to five weeks, any subjectivity in progress measurement does not have a significant effect on the cumulative position. Critical Path Analysis (CPA) on its own cannot do this as it only describes the critical activities as they are seen at that particular point in the project. Despite this, Critical Path Analysis (CPA) must not be ignored when assessing progress.

Forecasting

Forecasts use performance indices to predict the future. Based on past experience, we can say that the use of Earn Value Analysis can predict completion very accurately. In some cases it must be recognized that there will be a difference between 100 per cent completion and practical completion. Earn Value Analysis is better at predicting the former! In fact, even in one case where Earn value analysis was not as accurate as usual it was certainly closer than the predictions of the project team and was used to challenge their over optimism. By continuously plotting and reviewing trends, we identify problems earlier.

Corrective Action

The Project Management Consultant's interpretation of Earn Value Analysis has placed an emphasis on the use of man-days as the primary measure of program position. On the projects where this tool has been used, it has proved to be a more realistic measure than money for forecasting outcome in terms of time, particularly in the early stages of projects. The use of man-days also suggests corrective actions, and where appropriate recovery plans can be assessed as achievable or otherwise. For example, by simple calculation we determine the number of people required to complete on time.

Valuable Practice

The use of Earn Value Analysis demands the effective use of detailed plans, resourced plans and collection of progress reports, which are all things that professional Project Managers should be using in any event. These are valuable tools in their own right, but are prerequisites to use and benefit from Earn Value Analysis. In addition, efficiencies are realized, for example in assessing progress on site from a production perspective and separately assessing interim payments.

Where Earn Value Analysis has been used, it has brought together production, commercial and planning teams. Production staff has a direct influence on supplier's interim payments, including factoring in any quality issues, giving added authority to the people really needing it, those managing at the sharp end.

Estimating of Future Projects

As Earn Value Analysis imposes the requirement to record cost and effort expended, useful data is collected for use either in the estimating of future projects, or the validation of current plans. For example, if the number of man-hours expended for a certain trade in a past project is known, it is possible to estimate the requirements on current projects. This can prove very accurate provided that differing circumstances are considered. Historical information is a key to improving estimates.

Reduced Risk

Earn value analysis reduced risk because it enable realistic estimates of completion (for both cost and schedule) to be derived early in the project, it is possible to make adjustments and take necessary action to mitigate the risk of cost overruns and schedule slippage.

12.3 CREATING EARN VALUE ANALYSIS SYSTEM

There are two distinct phases in setting up an Earn Value Analysis system—the Planning Phase, and the Monitoring and Control, or Progress Monitoring Phase. In practice the two will often overlap, but are dealt with in turn below:

Project Definition and Planning Phase

Work Breakdown Structure

It breaks the project down into manageable discrete elements of work and may have several levels.

Each item in the work breakdown structure is generally assigned a unique identifier; these identifiers can provide a structure for hierarchical summation of cost and resources. It may be expressed in an organization chart format.

Creating such a structure is done when we create cost plans or sub-contract the work, but often the structures in different disciplines are not related. A formal Work Breakdown Structure (WBS) will demand this. It needs to be defined at least to the level that the project will be managed at—probably at supplier or trade level, but possibly also recognizing interim handovers, or discrete geographical definitions. It is greatly beneficial if this is done at the estimating stage, and if possible before Bills of Quantities or other pricing documents are produced. The output of these processes can then be used to inform the latter stages of setting up earn value analysis.

Scope Definition

Sub-dividing the major deliverables into smaller, more manageable components to provide better control. The work breakdown structure (WBS) breaks down the project into manageable pieces and the scope is then defined and developed against each item—this may be expressed on drawings, specifications and work content sheets. This step is a pre-requisite of the costing and planning of the project, not to mention procurement.

Planning/ Scheduling

In order to develop a schedule, one needs to define the activities, put them in order of how the work will be done (activity sequencing), and then estimate the duration of each activity (activity duration estimating).

The schedule should be logic linked and have the critical path and key milestones identified. Activity durations will ideally be in the 2-4 weeks range for construction activities, but there will exceptions. The critical point is that tasks should be clearly defined and described, and simple to assess progress against—not just for the Project Manager who puts the plan together but for those who will use and monitor it.

Costing

Costing are quantitative assessments of the likely cost of the resources to complete project activities. Costing may be done using a Bill of Quantities (BOQ) or pricing schedule. If it is possible to influence the production of the former i.e. with the early establishment of a work breakdown structure (WBS), it is useful to define how the bill will be split to reflect the program—this will obviously aid the costing of the schedule. Some forms of contract demand pricing against an Activity Schedule, which clearly should relate to a plan more readily than a traditional Bill of Quantities. Whatever tool has been used, once the costs have been established they are attributed to every activity on the schedule.

Resource Planning

Resource Planning may be a more extensive activity than you do on projects. Resource planning is the process of ascertaining future resource requirements for an organization or scope of work. The goal of resource planning is to ensure that labour, material, tools, consumable, which are often limited in availability or limited by density, are invested in a project over time in a way successfully, if not optimally, achieves project objective and requirements. Resourcing the plan ought to be a part of the planning-durations for activities cannot be derived without consideration of labour outputs. A plan without resources is no more than a statement of good intent—a resourced plan demonstrates the practicality of achieving the timescales shown. Provided that we spread the resources reasonably accurately, the total content is not important—our CPI will be used to adjust any over/under estimate when making projections or calculating recovery measures, and the SPI will be comparing like with like. Indeed, it is likely that our estimating of labour content will tend to be optimistic—and likely that our suppliers will be even more so. Information may also be requested from suppliers—and it may help them to be aware we will require this information before they price the work. It should therefore be a contract requirement that resourced and cost loaded programs will be required—but making this a contract requirement will not make obtaining this information any easier-experience has shown that the vigour with which it is pursued or insisted upon, rather than contract clauses that will determine how forthcoming it is! Whilst other measures can be used, there is a school of thought that the schedule ought to be measured with "deliverables", i.e. the physical output of the activity (e.g. numbers of pieces of equipment installed, or drawings produced on a design project). Projects are achieved by the expenditure of human effort, and recovery measures are based on this. The "deliverables" may however be used to assess progress.

12.4 MONITORING AND CONTROL PHASE

Baseline

A baseline schedule is a fixed project schedule and that is the standard by which project performance is measured. The "Working" schedule can continue to evolve and be developed; the baseline agreed for the contract remains the yardstick. Alterations to the baseline may be required as detail is developed—this development must not allow delay to be incorporated, unless there is a formal (client agreed) rebase line of the contract program (e.g. an Extension of Time).

Measurement of Progress

Measuring performance solely as a percentage complete has inherent risks. For example, if a task has a planned duration of eight days with twenty-five hours of work efforts, and four days have passed, typically, the performer will state that he is 50 per cent complete. The problem is that the Project Manager cannot tell from this estimate if the duration or the work effort is 50 per cent complete. As a best practice, several variables need to be considered—work effort expended, remaining work left to perform, and a re-assessment of remaining duration. By providing this variable, a more accurate percentage complete and an assessment of the schedule impact can be derived.

Assessments of project progress—should be done weekly and certainly no less than every other week as it becomes a regular routine—and supervisors should in any case be generally aware of the status of the works they are responsible for. Once it is a routine, the data is collected more reliably and quickly. Trends are evident earlier.

Collecting Actual Cost and Labour

The remaining pieces of information come from the labour returns and cost reports. Labour returns should be collected daily or weekly at worst, and collated to give a cumulative number of man-days by trade and an overall total. No attempt is made to allocate actual to a level lower than trade (or supplier) level—it would be onerous to do this accurately, for little reward. On the financial side, cost reports are generally produced monthly. This will coincide with the preparation of interim valuations for sub-contracted work.

Review and Action

Once we have made our progress assessment, Earn Value Analysis tool will automatically calculate our Earned Value (% complete × Budget for each activity). Various KPI's (Key Performance Index) can be calculated such as:

Cost Variance (CV)—The numerical difference between the earned value (BCWP) and the actual cost (ACWP). CV = BCWP – ACWP.

Schedule Variance (SV)—An indicator of how much a program is ahead of or behind schedule. SV = BCWP – BCWS. (Earned value-planned budget, or the difference between the value of work accomplished for a given period and the value of the work planned.) Schedule variance is presented well in chart format.

Cost Performance Index (CPI)—The cost efficiency factor representing the relationship between the actual cost expended and the earned value. CPI = BCWP/ACWP. A CPI ≥ 1 suggests a relatively efficient cost factor, while a CPI < 1 may be cause for concern.

Schedule Performance Index (SPI)—The planned schedule efficiency factor representing the relationship between the earned value and the initial planned schedule. SPI = BCWP/BCWS. A SPI ≥ 1 is good. SPI < 1 suggests actual work is falling behind the planned schedule.

Budget at Completion (BAC)—Original completion budget for project.

Estimate to Complete (ETC)—A calculated value, in dollars or hours that represents the cost of work required to complete remaining project tasks. ETC = BAC – BCWP.

Estimate at Complete (EAC)—A calculated value, in dollars or hours, that represents the projected total final costs of work when completed. EAC = ACWP + ETC. It is usual to review the progress report at a monthly meeting to decide where action needs to be taken. EVA will tell you where you have a problem, and what you need to do to finish the job on time, providing all stakeholders with a visibility of progress v/s plan.

Project Name:
Contract No.:
Period No.:

Date:
Completed By:

WBS Code	Element	Cost Variance	Schedule Variance	Cost CPI	Schedule SPI	ECTC	AFC	ETTC	OD	Forecast Additional Man-days
		CV = (EV – AC)	SV = (EV – PV)	CPI = (EV / AC)	SPI = (EV / PV)	ECTC = (CAB – EV) / CPI)	AFC = (CAB / CPI)	ETTC = OD / SPI		ETTC – OD
1.00	Pre-Pilot Plan	–4500.00	–5000.00	0.93	0.92	5388.00	67888.00	68.43	63.00	5.43
2.00	Checklists	1200.00	–16000.00	1.03	0.75	15600.00	62400.00	85.33	64.00	21.33
3.00	Curriculum	–3500.00	–3000.00	0.85	0.87	3525.00	27025.00	26.45	23.00	3.45
4.00	Mid-term Evaluation	–4500.00	0.00	0.94	1.00	–	72500.00	68.00	68.00	0.00
5.00	Implementation Support	0.00	–2000.00	1.00	0.83	2000.00	12000.00	14.40	12.00	2.40
6.00	Manual of Practice	200.00	–800.00	1.03	0.89	774.00	6774.00	7.90	7.00	0.90
7.00	Roll-out Plan	–4600.00	–6500.00	0.75	0.68	8715.00	26815.00	29.63	20.00	9.63
Totals		**–15700.00**	**–33300.00**	**6.53**	**5.94**	**36002.00**	**275402.00**	**300.14**	**257.00**	**43.14**

Earned Value Performance Report

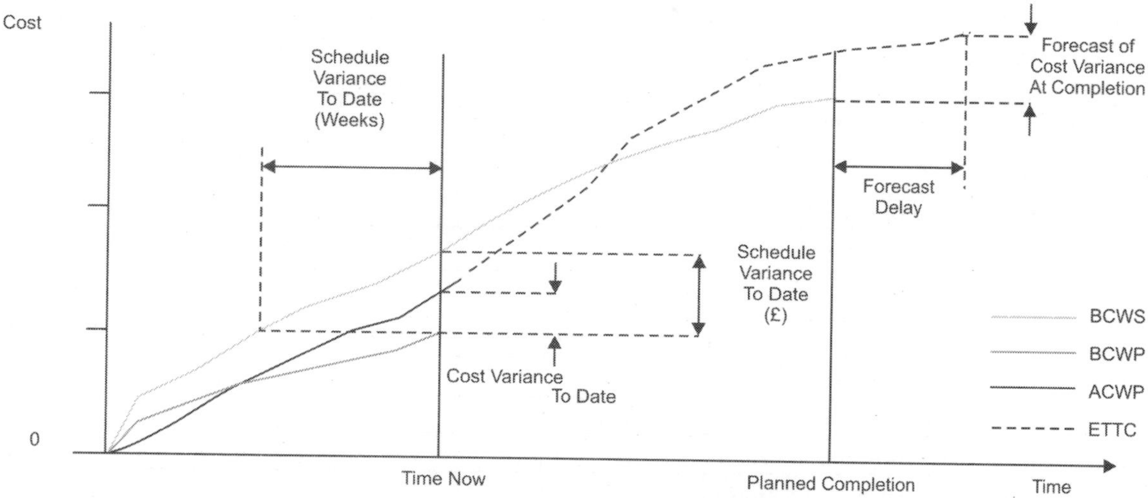

Earn Value Performance Graph

Change Control

It is possible to ignore variations if they do form a significant part of the project—the reflection in the cost performance index (CPI) will still give valuable information (not least to the client) about how the project is performing and likely out-turn costs. Even in this situation, any genuine changes of scope will probably require planning, and once this is accepted, the resourcing and costing work should follow. Minor variations (and we could debate whether these are genuinely variations or merely bits of scope that were not defined properly at the outset, or mistakes—perhaps in the design for example) can be rolled up and added to the schedule on a monthly or sub-contract basis (or both).

12.5 EVMS—RESPONSIBILITY MATRIX

P—Perform and Distribute Copies (As Noted) A—Approval (Original)

R—Review and Initial (Copy) D—Advise (Copy)

	Issues	Planning Dept.	Cost Control Dept.	Projects Control Manager	Project Manager	Top Management (GM and ND)	The Client
Input							
1	Work Breakdown Structure (WBS) Element Code	P	P	R	R & A	–	–
2	WBS Element Description	P	P	R	R & A	–	–
3	Program	P	–	R	R & A	D	D
4	Planned Budget Amount (Cost/Man-hours)	P	P	R	R & A	D	D
5	Actual (Cost/Man-hours)	P	P	R	R & A	–	–
Output (Based on Cost)							
1	Earned Value	–	P	R	R & A	–	–
2	Cost Variance (CV)	–	P	R	R & A	–	–
3	Cost Performance Index (CPI)	–	P	R	R & A	–	–
4	Schedule Performance Index (SPI)	–	P	R	R & A	–	–
5	Estimated Cost to Complete (ECTC)	–	P	R	R & A	–	–
6	Estimate (cost) at Completion (EAC) or Anticipated Final Cost (AFC)	–	P	R	R & A	–	–
7	Earned Value Performance Reports	–	P	R	R & A	D	D
Output (Based on Man-hours)							
1	Earned Value	P	–	R	R & A	–	–
2	Schedule Variance (SV)	P	–	R	R & A	–	–
3	Cost Performance Index (CPI)	P	–	R	R & A	–	–
4	Schedule Performance Index (SPI)	P	–	R	R & A	–	–
5	Estimated Man-hour to Complete (ECTC)	P	–	R	R & A	–	–
6	Estimate (Man-hour) at Completion (EAC) or Anticipated Final Man-hour (AFC)	P	–	R	R & A	–	–
7	Earned Value Performance Reports	P	–	R	R & A	D	D

Quality Control and Assurance

13

13.1 INTRODUCTION

Quality Control: Once the Architects and Engineers have set the criteria for construction, quality control ensures that the physical work conforms to those standards.

This process includes:

(1) Setting specific standards for construction performance, usually through the plans and specifications.

(2) Measuring variances from the standards.

(3) Taking action to correct or minimize adverse variance and standards.

(4) Planning for improvements in the standards themselves and in conformance with the standards.

Quality Assurance: Although its definition is not well standardized, quality assurance is generally a broader, more nearly all-encompassing term for the application of standards and procedures to ensure that a product or a facility meets or exceeds desired performance criteria. It also usually includes the documentation necessary to verify that all steps in the procedures have been satisfactorily completed. The term transcends both quality engineering and quality control, where in the first phase, it includes the design of a product whose quality is economical in terms of its end use, and in the second, it includes the development and application of procedures which will, at economical levels, assure attainment of the designed quality.

13.2 THE QUALITY SYSTEM

Basic elements of quality include:

- Quality characteristics such as concrete compressive strength, slump, size of aggregate, ratio of water to cement, surface finish and sometimes the colour.
- Quality of design that specify not only the desired standard for the characteristics that define a product but also tolerances and ranges for acceptable variations from the standard such as concrete rebar spacing, and percentage of compressive strength cylinders that break below the value.
- Quality of conformance which is the degree to which the physical work produced conforms to the standard.

All the elements of quality combine to determine the quality of the final product. The owner's needs are expressed in the design criteria that guide the engineering and design process that produces the technical specifications for the project. This in effect sets the quality of design.

The quality of conformance is influenced by:

- The actual field construction methods, includes the skill of the workers, the capabilities of their tools and equipment, and the quality of their raw materials;
- The supervision they receive and the managerial controls that are applied to direct the workers in accordance with the plans and specifications; and
- The inspection and quality control procedures that are applied, including the knowledge and skill of the inspectors and the reliability of their methods and tools for measuring the quality characteristics specified by the designers.

Quality of design and quality of conformance, in turn, determine the quality of the constructed facility.

13.3 THE PROJECT CONTROL ROLE IN THE QUALITY PROGRAM

The PM team must satisfy itself that the construction complies with the design specifications to include applicable local regulatory and statutory requirements.

The requirement for formally certified tests and inspections are presented in the individual project specifications. A matrix for responsibility and authority must be developed early in the project to manage the inspection and test requirements of each works package. This information should be included in the requirements of each of the relevant Contractors Project Management Plans whose work is subject to test.

The Contractor's Project Management Plans including the Inspection and Test Plan should be approved before the Contractor commences work and should have been reviewed by PM Team, the Design Team and the Client and if necessary, amended before testing and inspection commences.

Following the successful completion of Certification Testing, the originals of all test certificates must be forwarded for safe-keeping to the nominated member of the Design Team and Planning Supervisor for inclusion in the quality assurance files. A full set of copies will be held by the document controller and filed by Contractor.

After Contractors complete sections of their work including 100% clearance of snags, they will offer the works, to the best of their knowledge and as a result of 100% checking, defect free, to PM Team.

A final inspection and sign off regime will be agreed between PM Team, the Design Team, the Client and any other interested parties or authorities.

The PM Team Manager is responsible for the defect clearance process and as such, must determine:

Who should witness/inspect
Who should sign
Notice periods
Procedures and authority for checking rework

The PM Team must emphasize to all inspectors that:

Notwithstanding the PM policy to meet or exceed the requirements of the specification, any work that satisfies the specification or documented changes is correct.

Any additional works or changes to specification identified during these inspections will be treated as defects and must be treated as additional works including the issue of relevant instructions and acceptance of time and cost variations.

"Meeting customer requirements is very important."

Comparison Between Standard Form of Construction Contract

14

14.1 INTRODUCTION

NEC (New Engineering Contract)

The NEC is a modern day family of standard contracts that truly embrace the concept of partnership and encourages Employers, Designers, Contractors and Project Managers to work together through both, a powerful management tool and a legal framework to facilitate all aspects of the creation of construction projects.

The NEC is a legal framework of Project Management procedures designed to handle all aspects of the management of engineering and construction projects.

- NEC is suite of contracts the most commonly used of which is the Engineering and Construction Contract (ECC) the main contract form used an Employer to engage a main contractor.

Its principle benefits are:

Flexibility—It is a modular form of contract with a choice of pricing options and risk allocation coupled with a series of secondary options which can be used to tailor the contract to suit project specific requirements. Design responsibility can also reside with either party in whole or in part.

Clarity and Simplicity—Written in ordinary language, with limited use of legal terminology, simple lines of communication and the use of subjective decisions minimized.

Facilitator of Effective Project Management—The contract is a management tool which drives clear and timely decision-making; clearly allocates responsibility and drives the foresighted management of risk and change.

Encourages Collaborative Working—The contract requires the parties to operate in a "Spirit of mutual trust and cooperation".

SUITE OF CONTRACTS

NEC is a suite of contracts containing the following contracts:

- NEC3 Engineering and Construction Contract (ECC) (June 2005)
- NEC3 Engineering and Construction Sub-contract (ECS) (June 2005)
- NEC3 Engineering and Construction Short Sub-contract (June 2005)
- NEC3 Professional Services Contract (PSC) (June 2005)
- NEC3 Engineering and Construction Short Contract (ECSC) (June 2005)

- NEC3 Adjudicator's Contract (AC) (June 2005)
- NEC3 Term Service Contract (June 2005)
- NEC3 Framework Contract (FC) (June 2005)

The most commonly used contract is the ECC which is the main contract form used by an Employer to engage a main Contractor.

The ECC consists of six main options, one of which has to be selected by the Client prior to tender and which allocate the financial risk between the parties and the method of reimbursement to the Contractor.

There is no design and build option as all of the above options allow for any allocation of design responsibility.

PPC INTERNATIONAL (PROJECT PARTNERING CONTRACT)

This is the first standard form of Project Partnering Contract designed to underpin a team-based approach and to promote clarity and confidence among Partnering Team members. PPC International allows the Client, the Contractor, all key specialist Consultants and Sub-contractors and suppliers to sign a single Partnering Contract. Therefore, there is no need for separate appointment contracts for the Contractor, Consultants, Sub-contractors, etc.

PPC International takes the mystery out of project partnering by mapping the way that a partnering team really works. It aligns contractual project management processes with teamwork methods and behaviours.

PPC International integrates the design, supply and construction process from inception to completion by setting up a practical and clear basis for all the key players to work together, according to agreed timetables, from early design right through to commissioning and handover.

PPC International underpins trust and co-operation by bringing together Clients, Contractors, Consultants and Specialist into a single contractual hub allowing all the team members to "contract as a team" on identical terms.

PPC International enables better inputs from constructors, consultants and specialist by involving them as "signed-up" members of the team, early enough in the pre-construction phase to add real value to the project.

SUITE OF CONTRACTS

PPC International—ACA Standard Form of Project Partnering Contract (contains contracts for engagement of Contractors, Consultants, Sub-contractors).

SPC 2000—ACA Standard Form of Specialist Contract Project Partnering (contains provisions for appointing specialist sub-contractors and should be used under PPC International).

FIDIC

FIDIC is a body that has been producing standard forms of construction contracts since 1957.

The contracts are of a traditional nature and have their roots in the Institution of Civil Engineers standard forms of contract. They are well established and are one of the most commonly used forms on an International basis.

Independently produced and designed to form an equitable allocation of risk between the Parties. Well established and very familiar to Employer and Contractors. Designed for International use. A suite of contracts is available.

FIDIC issued the latest edition of its contracts in 1999.

SUITE OF CONTRACTS

- Red Book—Conditions of Contract for Construction
- Silver Book—Conditions of Contract for EPC / Turnkey Projects
- Yellow Book—The Plant and Design-Build Contract
- Short Form Contract
- The White Book—Client / Consultancy Agreement
- Construction Contract MDB Harmonized (2006 World Bank Projects)
- Dredgers Contract (2006)
- Gold Book—Design Build Operate Contacts (2006).

14.1.1 Key Differences

Collaboration

ECC

Creates a bi-party partnering arrangement between the Employer and Contractor and requires the parties to work together in a spirit of mutual trust and co-operation. Also, through the use of the optional X12, the partnering agreement can be extended to encompass other members of the construction team by creating a core group and shared set of KPI's but it does not create any contractual link between these wider parties.

PPC INTERNATIONAL

Creates a multiparty partnering agreement with all members of the construction team (Client, contractor, sub-contractors, consultants) employed under the same contract and therefore, the same contract terms. PPC International contains a Project Partnering Agreement which sets the scene for successful partnering from day one.

FIDIC

FIDIC does not specifically refer to partnering and there is no partnering agreement of charter within the contracts. There is also no ability to link together the performance of separate members of the construction team.

Design Responsibility

ECC

The ECC allows any allocation of design responsibility between the parties from full design and build to construct only.

PPC INTERNATIONAL

PPC International allows any allocation of design responsibility between the parties to the contract including the Client, Contactor and Consultants.

FIDIC

Differing FIDIC forms allocate differing design responsibility on the parties:

- Red Book—majority Employer designed
- Silver Book EPC / Turnkey—full Contractor design
- Yellow Book Design and Build—Contractor will do most of the design.

Parties to the Contract

ECC

A bi-party agreement between Employer and Contractor.

PPC INTERNATIONAL

A multiparty agreement between Employer, Contractor, Consultant and Sub-contractors. As new members join the construction team, they are added to the contract or replaced as they leave.

FIDIC

A bi-party agreement between Employer and Contractor.

Pricing Options

ECC

The ECC has a choice of pricing options detailed below:

- Option A: Priced contract with activity schedule (Fixed Price, Lump sum)
- Option B: Priced contract with bill of quantities (re-measurable)
- Option C: Target contract with activity schedule (target cost vs. actual cost)
- Option D: Target contract with bill of quantities (target cost vs. actual cost)
- Option E: Cost reimbursable contract (actual cost)
- Option F: Management contract (actual cost of works package contractors).

PPC INTERNATIONAL

There is no initial lump price option under PPC International as the Contractor is engaged prior to finalization of the design, however, one can be developed and agreed as prior to commencement of construction works on site.

The price is essentially based on prime cost, which comprises sub-contracts and direct labour packages plus amounts specified in the price framework for the Contractor's profit, head office and site overheads.

FIDIC

FIDIC provides a choice of payment options depending on which contract is selected.

- Red Book is generally based on a Bill of Quantities and is re-measurable, however, it is common for Employers to amend this to make the contract a fixed price lump sum
- Silver Book EPC—fixed price lump sum
- Yellow Book—fixed price lump sum

Pre-construction Services/ Early Contractor Involvement

ECC

The ECC does not contain any specific provisions for pre-construction works or early contractor involvement (ECI).

The NEC suite is however, commonly used for ECI projects with either the Professional Services Contract being used to engage the Contractor during the pre-construction stage or using the ECC (normally Option E Cost Reimbursable) in a two-stage process whereby an initial contract is awarded for the pre-construction stage/enabling works followed by the negotiation/agreement of a price for the construction phase.

PPC INTERNATIONAL

PPC International specifically provides for the early selection of the Project Partnering Team and the collaborative finalization of designs, prices and members of the supply chain.

FIDIC

FIDIC does not contain any specific provisions for pre-construction works or early contractor involvement (ECI). The FIDIC contracts are however, used for ECI projects with either the FIDIC Short Form being used to engage the Contractor during the pre-construction stage/enabling works or using the Red Book in a two-stage process whereby an initial contract is awarded for the pre-construction stage/enabling works followed by the negotiation/agreement of a price for the construction phase.

Speed to Site

ECC

The differing main pricing options allow varying speeds to site through the overlap of design with construction and the removal of the requirement to negotiate a fixed price.

The flexible allocation of design responsibility under all the ECC main options allows an earlier start on site if design responsibility is passed to the Contractor. Even with full Employers design, the target cost options allows a quicker start on site as the project does not have to be fully specified for a target cost to be agreed. Under Option E Cost Reimbursable and Option F Management Contracting an almost immediate start on site can be achieved as there is no requirement to agree a scope of works and price prior to construction.

PPC INTERNATIONAL

As PPC International specifically provides for the early selection of the Project Partnering Team an earlier start on site can be achieved than under a traditional lump sum form of contract. This is also assisted by the fact that a fixed price is not agreed and the price for the works can be developed as the design progresses and packages of work are let.

FIDIC

The FIDIC Red Book is either re-measurable based on Bills of Quantities or fixed price lump sum and does not lend itself to an early start on site.

If the Silver (EPC) or Yellow (design and build) contracts are selected, then some element of overlap between design and construction can be achieved.

Risk/Variations

ECC

The ECC is sometimes perceived as a Contractor friendly contract. The drafters however, would argue that it simply provides a fair allocation of risk. In reality, the vast majority of issues which constitute compensation events (variations in ECC terminology) under the ECC would also constitute variations under nearly all other forms of contract. The key difference with the ECC is that all compensation events allow the Contractor to claim more time and money and there are no neutral events. This also extends to force majeure issues.

PPC INTERNATIONAL

Under PPC International, the Partnering Team members determine the allocation of risk between themselves, with the exception of a Client change which always remains with the Employer. There are in effect six neutral events under PPC International which gives rise to an extension of time to the Contractor but with no additional claim for the cost of site based overheads.

FIDIC

FIDIC has a very traditional approach to risk allocation and contains most of the variation headings expected under the majority of standard forms. There are two neutral events under FIDIC that entitle the Contractor to an extension of time but no additional costs and a further four grounds for an extension of time and an increase in cost but no profit recovery by the Contractor.

Program

ECC

Under the ECC, the program is a contract document and is of fundamental importance. There are extensive and some may say onerous requirements for the format and content of the program. These are far in excess of the requirements in other standard forms of contract. The contract also requires for the program to be continually updated to reflect the actual progress achieved and the effects of extensions of time.

PPC INTERNATIONAL

PPC International contains a Partnering Time-table which governs the activities of the Partnering Team members prior to commencement on site. There is also a Project Time-table which governs the activities of the Partnering Team members during the construction phase.

FIDIC

The FIDIC forms contain a basic obligation on the Contractor to provide a program and covers some of the issues it is required to cover, but does not go into detail. There is also no obligation for the program to be regularly updated and re-submitted to the Employer.

Key Performance Indicators

ECC

The ECC contains two secondary options which allow the introduction of Key Performance Indicators. The content and performance levels in the KPI's is to be determined by the Employer and if the Contractor better the levels they will be entitled to a bonus payment. If they fail to achieve the levels, the Contractor will be required to improve but will not suffer any financial penalty.

PPC INTERNATIONAL

Under PPC International, Key Performance Indicators are part of the core contract. The content and performance levels in the KPI's are determined by the Partnering Team members. Payments to the Partnering Team members can then be linked to these KPIs.

FIDIC

KPI's do not feature in standard FIDIC contracts.

Proactive Management and Early Warnings

ECC

Unlike most contract forms which deal with issues respectively, the ECC takes a fundamentally different approach and requires the parties to proactively manage the contract. The parties are required to work together and to openly share problems and risks as soon as they become aware of them. The parties are then required to work together in a "spirit of mutual trust and cooperation" to seek solutions to these issues and to mitigate their impact on all those effected. The ECC contains an early warning mechanism, which requires either party to inform the other of any issue that is or may effect time, cost or quality. The notification is then followed by a meeting at which the parties co-operate to solve the problem and agree a way forward.

The ECC requires all changes to time and cost, consequent upon compensation events occurring (ECC terminology for variations), to be assessed contemporaneously with the events arising and preferably before change is instructed. The intention is that these project management procedures enable the parties to successfully manage risk and give the employer greater choice and control over change management together with greater time and cost certainty. If the contractual mechanism is fully implemented, the effect of all changes should have been agreed prior to or within weeks of the completion date, allowing the final account value to be determined contemporaneously with completion.

PPC INTERNATIONAL

PPC International has a similar approach to pro-active management as the ECC. It also requires the parties to work together to identify and openly share problems and risks as soon as they become aware of them. The parties are then required to work together in to seek solutions to these issues and to mitigate their impact on all those affected.

PPC International also contains an early warning mechanism, which requires either party to inform the other of any issue that is or may effect time, cost or quality. The notification is then followed by a meeting at which the parties co-operate to solve the problem and agree a way forward. PPC International encourages the effects of change to be agreed in advance but does allow certain changes to be instructed and for their evaluation to follow later.

FIDIC

FIDIC takes a traditional approach to contract administration. Whilst it does encourage the parties to agree the effects of change in advance, it recognizes that the parties may not achieve this and has provisions to retrospectively agree the effects of change and agree a final account at the end of a project to "wrap up" all the outstanding issues.

There are no early warning provisions under FIDIC forms.

Management Requirements

ECC

The ECC is not only a set of terms and conditions but also a set of management processes. These management requirements are generally in excess of what is required under other standard contract forms at least in terms of contract administration as opposed to good project management principles which will be the same regardless of contract form.

Therefore, to effectively manage an ECC contract in accordance with the contractual procedures and timescales will require a greater level of management resource than required under other standard forms.

PPC INTERNATIONAL

PPC International tries to stimulate pro-active management of the contract and in particular, the effective and timely management of change. The level of management requirements will generally be greater than those required under standard contract forms and PPC International also create the additional role of Partnering Advisor who is engaged to ensure all the parties fulfil their obligations and can provide an additional facility for problem resolution.

FIDIC

FIDIC has a traditional approach to the management of construction projects and the level of resources required to effectively manage the contract are comparable with other similar standard forms of contract.

"The types of work or goods being procured dictate the appropriate contract type."

Delay and Disruptions

15

15.1 INTRODUCTION

Delays and disruptions are two separate things. Delay is lateness and disruption is loss of productivity, disturbance, hindrance or interruption to progress.

The purpose of this procedure is to avoid disputes (that have to be decided by the third parties such as adjudicators, dispute review boards, arbitrators, judges, etc.) by a proper approach to understanding in the preparation and evaluation of claims due to delays and disruptions in construction industry.

At the outset of a contract, it is helpful if the Contractor and the Engineer ensure that those responsible for administering the Contract have a clear understanding of each other's role and responsibilities, and to what extent they may be governed, or limited by:

(i) The terms and conditions of the Contract—the terms of engagement between the Employer and the Engineer—delegated powers.

(ii) The Contractor's management structure/company policy.

The contract and written letters confirming the scope of delegation should satisfy, however discussion at the outset to air views on any matters which may facilitate better communication and avoid misunderstandings between the parties that can only be beneficial to all concerned.

The Engineer should recognize that the Contractor is in business to make a profit, and it owes a duty to its shareholders to do so. Any act or omission by the Engineer which affects the Contractor's progress will naturally be treated by the Contractor as good grounds for a claim. The Engineer owes a duty of care to both the Contractor and the Employer and must therefore deal with these matters honestly and fairly.

On the other hand, the Contractor should recognize that the Engineer, having certain powers and obligations under the Contract and a duty of care to both the Employer and the Contractor, is likely to be shot at from both sides. In case disagreement on any matters, each should try to approach the problem from the other's point of view.

15.2 RECORDS AND INFORMATION NECESSARY FOR EVALUATION OF CLAIM

Proper evaluation of claims can best be achieved if the Contractor and the Engineer recognize the events or circumstances which may give rise to a claim at the earliest possible time, and that they are dealt with as soon as practicable.

The Contractor should, as a matter of course and whether or not a claim should arise, prepare suitable information and keep contemporary records. Records and information which are likely to be of most use in the formulation and settlement of claims (or for the preparation of pleadings and evidence for arbitration, in the event that claims cannot be settled), are:

A master program indicating how the Contractor had envisaged the sequence and timing of the various activities based on the tender (or pre-contract) information and any updates in accordance with events which may occur during the progress of the:

- A progress schedule to compare progress of the various activities against the master program.
- An estimate of resources and anticipated expenditure each week, or month, required to comply with the master program.
- Records of actual resources and actual expenditure based on progress
- Records of plant standing or un-economically employed
- Records of overtime worked, and the cost thereof
- Progress photographs
- Drawing register (annotated to give details of amendments)
- Site diaries

Notes kept at meetings.

It is self-evident that the more organized the Contractor's approach to the keeping of records, the easier will be the Engineer's task. The absence of good records should not bar a valid claim, and subject to compliance with the notice provisions, the Engineer is bound to make his own evaluation of a claim, despite the shortcomings of the records and documentation placed before him.

15.3 PROLONGATION COST

The principle behind a claim for prolongation costs are simply that due to one single act e.g. an Engineer's Order to suspend the progress of the Works or any part thereof, or due to several different events and circumstances, the aggregate effect of which has caused the period for completion of the Works to be extended, the Contractor has remained on site and expended resources over a long period. In the normal course of events, the Contractor would have spent considerably more sums of money in managing and carrying out the work than it would have done had there been no extended period. The Contractor is entitled to complete before the original date for completion, and this should be taken into account when determining the total prolongation period.

15.4 HEADS OF CLAIM FOR RECOVERY OF PROLONGATION COSTS

1. Overheads

(a) Head Office Overheads

Head Office Overheads will need to be considered in the light of the accounting principles adopted by the Contractor. If the cost of senior management and head office clerical staffs are charged to the job, it will be easier to establish this as a cost incurred by the Contractor in managing and carrying out the works.

If the Contractor does not charge the cost of senior management and clerical staff to the job, then the cost (plus all other relevant Head Office costs), may be allocated on a proportional basis over the period. The well established "Hudson Formula" is usually accepted as a means of calculating the additional Head Office Overheads over the period, i.e.

$$\frac{\text{Overheads percentage}}{100} \times \frac{\text{Contract Sum}}{\text{Contract Period}} \times \text{Period of Delay}$$

Various other important Formulas for Head Office Overheads are Emden Formula, Eichleay Formula and Hank Laan Formula.

There are grounds to argue that some of the Head Office Overhead costs would have been incurred whether or not there had been any prolongation, and as such, the formula represents a calculation of the possible loss to the Contractor that it may have earned, to cover its overheads elsewhere had there been no delay. In order to resist the above argument, the Contractor should ensure that the calculation of the overheads percentage reflects those costs which could reasonably be said to be expenditure necessary to manage and carry out the works. The following guidelines may be useful in meeting this objective:

(a) Extract all items from the annual accounts (over a period which spans the total contract period, including the prolonged period) which are relevant to the operating costs of construction. In order to do this, the annual costs of marketing, publicity, staff training, staff recruitment and the like may have to be deducted from the total overhead costs since they are costs which would generally have been incurred irrespective of the delay. If any of these costs were incurred in respect of the job, these should be dealt with separately.

(b) If finance charges are incurred to enable the company to operate, and if these appear in the accounts as overheads, exclude these from the calculations since they may not have been incurred in connection with the job.

(b) Site Overheads

The Contractor's Site Overhead costs those are most likely to be eligible for including in a claim for prolongation are:

(i) Supervision	– Salary
	– Bonus/gratuity
	– Accommodation
	– Pensions
	– Statutory payments
(ii) Site offices	– Rental or depreciation
	– Repairs and maintenance
(iii) Services	– Heating
	– Air conditioning/lighting
	– Telephone/telex
	– Water

(iv) Plant/transport
- Tractors
- Browsers/dumpers
- Silos/general site mixing plant
- Small tools and equipments

(v) Miscellaneous
- Insurance
- Bond premiums

Due to the fact that the monthly costs of the above items are likely to vary, it is not appropriate to use a formula (e.g. Hudson or Eichleay), nor is it appropriate to claim the cost of Site Overheads for the period between the original Completion date and the prolonged Completion date. If it is possible to consider a period of delay in isolation, e.g. a period of suspension, then the monthly costs applicable to the period of suspension should normally be taken as the basis of calculation. If the period of prolongation has been the result of several causes of delay, each cause being a contributory factor to the overall period of prolongation, but being impossible to disentangle so as to consider each cause separately, then it will be necessary to establish the period(s) during which the total delay(s) occurred, and apply the appropriate monthly costs to the period(s) of delay which caused the prolongation.

2. Inflation

A secondary affect of prolongation is usually to cause all or a substantial part of the works to be carried out at times which were later than the original program. The Contractor would be carrying out work progressively later as each cause of delay added to the effects of previous delays. Consequently, any increase in the cost of labour and/or materials which occurred during the life of the contract would have an increasing effect on the cost of carrying out the woks, and as such, should be recoverable as part of the prolongation costs.

In order to evaluate the effects of inflation on construction costs, it is necessary to compare the actual effects of inflation on the work (as carried out) with the theoretical effects of inflation which would otherwise have occurred if the Contractor had carried out the work in accordance with the original program.

15.5 DISRUPTION COST

In order to make a claim for the costs of disruption, it must be evident that some pre-planned or orderly sequence of work had been affected by an act of the Employer, or Engineer and/or by a variation or number of variations, so that the actual sequence is different from the planned or orderly sequence. Wholesale disruption may also bring about prolongation and its associated cost. It is often the case that individual sections of work are affected in a way which does not, by themselves, cause prolongation but are, nevertheless, substitute to additional cost.

The prime questions to be addressed are:

1. What work was affected?
2. How was it affected?
3. With what should the action progress and cost be compared, in order to assess the additional cost?

15.6 HEADS OF CLAIM FOR RECOVERY OF DISRUPTION COSTS

Plant, Tools and Equipment

Disruption may cause uneconomical use of plant, idling time, change of the type of plant, etc. Is the plant owned by the Contractor, or is it hired? Was it necessary to retain the plant or equipment on site, or should it have been removed from site and subsequently returned?

Loss of Productivity

It is preferable to deal with each section of work separately, comparing actual productivity with productivity which ought to have been achieved on similar work. The Contractor's tender may be a suitable base. However, it is often necessary to make comparisons with several published texts or manufactures literature for plant. If possible, comparison with a similar section of work on the same job (which was not disrupted) would produce additional information for assessment.

Re-deployment of Workmen

Particularly, if disrupted work causes peaks or valley in the Contractor's workforce, it may be necessary to re-deploy workmen from other contracts or engage additional Sub-Contractors at higher rates causing costs of travelling, lodging, visas, etc. to be incurred. Re-deployment of labour from one part of the site to another may cause secondary disruption that cannot be avoided in the overall interests of the job.

15.7 ADDITIONAL PRELIMINARY

The Contractor may price every item of preliminaries in a separate section of the Bill of Quantities set out for this purpose, or it may price some or all of the preliminaries in the rates. Different pricing policies create different problems when it comes to dealing with the evaluation of additional preliminaries which may be due as a result of delay and/or variations.

A considerable proportion of the additional preliminaries may be recovered in a claim for prolongation.

There are, however, other reasons for adjustments to be made to properly recover additional preliminaries, whether or not there has been a delay.

The ordering of a variation may require the Contractor to incur costs on preliminary items which have not been recovered in the rates. A variation for additional work may necessitate bringing on to site a survey team, supervisors and accommodation to set out and oversee the execution of the works included in the variation. The Contractor's rates for executing the additional work may be appropriate in respect of the measured work, but the rates may not be built up to include the preliminary items which the Contractor would not have incurred if the works had not been ordered. Such costs plus profit should be included in the total evaluation of the variation taken into account in ascertaining the amount of the Contract Price.

It will be of some assistance to Engineers and Contractors if the total cost (or value) of preliminaries is broken down into the following three categories:

(i) Time related

(ii) Method related

(iii) Value related

(i) and (ii) may be difficult to deal with in the absence of clear definitions because the two categories are often inter-related so as to be almost impossible to disentangle. A common sense approach to this problem is necessary if a reasonable evaluation is to be achieved. There are, however, several items which would normally fall under category (i) and should not present much difficulty.

(iii) Insurances tend to be value related as well as being time related particularly if the underwriters require premiums to be re-calculated on the final value of the works or on the actual cost of labour for Employer's Liability Insurances. If additional insurance premiums become payable as a result of increase in the value of the works, the evaluation of the amount due to the Contractor should be straightforward. If additional insurance premiums become payable as a result of the actual cost of the payroll, then it may be necessary to ascertain why the extra labour costs were incurred and to make a distinction between inefficiency, under-estimation at tender stage, disruption and uneconomic working and changes in method caused by variations.

15.8 CLAIM PRESENTATION

Introduction: Contract Particulars

Identifying the parties to the contract, describing the works, giving details of tender and acceptance, identifying the form of contract and amendments, the contract sum; planned/actual completion, liquidated damages; the program.

Summary of Facts

Dates of commencement and practical completion summarize notification/application for E.O.T., E.O.T. awards, claims submitted, final account, claims assessed to date, amount of latest certificate and retention, payments received.

Basis of Claim

Contract condition/provisions applicable, common law provisions, contractual analysis and explain basis for claim.

Details of Claim

A logical format, setting out key dates, events, causes, effects, reference to contract documents/drawings, bills, specification, conditions of contract.

With full narrative on the circumstances of each delay, it affects on progress, cost implication and completion. It is stressed that clear distinction between cause and effect must be established and distinguished between extension of time and the financial effects of delay/and disruption.

Evaluation of Claim

Calculation of each head of claim with reasoning and methods for calculation with substantiating evidence where necessary.

Statement of Claim

Setting out claimant's entitlements including as yet unpaid retention monies, valuations and re-measured works as yet unpaid including variations, also noting that all finance charges accrue until settlement.

It is always better to settle the claims at the earliest, unresolved claims will become harder and more expensive to resolve in the later stage. By knowing the requirements of evaluation, methods of calculations, claim presentation, etc. as detailed in this chapter, it is easy to settle the claims most efficiently and quickly.

15.9 CLAIM STATUS REPORT LOG

CLAIM STATUS REPORT LOG

Period Ending:

No.	Type of Claim	Contractor's Claim				PM's Adjudication					Payment Status				Employer's Approval	Remarks
		Ref.	Date	Days	Amount	Ref.	Date	Days	Amount	For Period Up to	Date	Payment No.	Gross Claimed	Certified Amount		
	Totals															

Sample

Project Close-out

16

16.1 INTRODUCTION

The purpose of this chapter is to present an overview of the guidelines that allow the smooth handover of the project and all relevant deliverables to the Client and provide feedback information for continuous improvement on other projects. It is important that the completion phase is handled in a controlled and disciplined manner. The completion phase starts with the defect clearance, testing and commissioning and ends only when the Final Account has been closed.

The Project Management Schedule should include sufficient time subsequent to the completion of construction works to allow for a proper close-out period. Staff Levels should be planned to ensure adequate staff personnel remain throughout the construction and contractor demobilization periods to provide sufficient workforce to complete the PM Team obligations.

16.2 COMPLETION OF CONTRACTS

Tests and Inspection

Satisfy itself that the construction complies with the design specifications to include applicable local regulatory and statutory requirements.

Defect Clearance

A final inspection and sign off procedure including assignment of responsibilities will be agreed between the PM Team, the Design Team, the Client and any other interested parties or authorities.

As-Built Drawings and O&M Manuals

These documents are retained for eventual transfer to the Client for its permanent archives and use.

Handover/Practical Completion

Any agreed outstanding items should be documented and their clearance be closed out as early as in convenient to the Client/end user.

Safety

The site must be inspected on completion to ensure that no safety hazards remain. For example, blocked fire escapes, unguarded smoke vent shafts, weak duct floors, etc. We must not knowingly leave safety hazards, even if they are part of the design. The Safety Department must be consulted if any doubt exists.

Defects Liability Period

The main form of corporate reporting employed during this period is the Maintenance and Final Account Report occasionally supplemented by the monthly report.

RECORD RETENTION

Archive the following documents on Project:

- Proposal Documents
- Contract Documents
- Contract documents including drawings and specifications
- As-Built documents including drawings and specifications
- Change documents
- Schedule documents
- Payment documents
- Drawing Register
- Correspondence Files
- Minutes of Meetings
- Quality Records
- Safety Records
- Trade Contract Documents
- All Final Account Statements

The following should be carried out in accordance with agreed procedure:

Trade Contractor Ratings

The quality of information for tender lists from the Procurement Department for future work is dependent upon good and regular feedback from existing contracts.

Feedback is gained by all Project completion the Company Rating Report issued by the Procurement Department. If one has not been issued to the team before completion, its issue should be requested.

The company Rating Report should be completed by the team members most qualified for each discipline and not necessarily the recipient.

The need for safety information which related to Contractor competence arises from the Client and local safety legislation.

Contracts Closing Sheet/Quality Management Close-out

When work on site has been completed, the Project Manager shall prepare the Contract Closing Sheet/Quality Management Close-out Form.

"Closing a project is the ideal opportunity for capturing lessons learned and facilitating knowledge transfer."

16.3 LESSONS LEARNED (SAMPLE)

Category	Problem	Impact	Solution	Ranking	Comments	Assoc docs	Author
Construction	Non-certified animal translocation companies engaged to undertake the works.	No grading can commence until animal translocation properly certified.	Translocation contractor engaged as certified by the government	High	Ensure correct certified paperwork is presented during tender negotiations.		X
Commercial	Certain areas required to be graded as a priority but not defined as a milestone under the contract.	Request to grade nominated plots became a potential variation due to loss of rate of work as continuity is not maintained through numerous relocation of plant.	Program was re-sequenced to take into account priority areas and maintain countinuity of work. Close communication upheld between client, PM, Engineer and Contractor.	High	Review priority areas at an design stage and make provisions in the contract for some late provision/request.		X
HSE	Random movement of large machinery in a potentially poor visibility site with foot traffic.	High risk of an accident causing injury to pedestrians.	Clear routes defined for heavy machinery including drop off and waiting areas for pedestrians.	High	Traffic management plan for plant and pedestrians to be submitted prior to start.		X
Construction	Access routes continuously altered due to grading works	Change in routes causes confusion on site and additional time and cost incured due to each alteration.	Contractors temporary access routes coordinated to be in line with future roadways where possible	Low	Grading contractor to be provided with future road layout to ensure co-ordination of temp roads with final.		X
Construction	Site accessed and site traffic movement not controlled.	No proper traffic order on site. Damage caused to graded plots and R&I work in progress.	Provide phased completed main strategic traffic routes to key areas within the development	High	Timely completion of main road including lighting provides the development with easily managed traffic control and good advertising for the client that progress is underway		X
Design	Part of development boundary not clearly defined and agreed to by all authorities.	Work partially undertaken in the concerned areas was put on hold, causing potential delays and abortive works.	Whole works reviewed and put on hold where potential impacts may occur. Project re-sequenced to avoid impacted areas until the end.	High	Review to be undertaken during the design stage to ensure all boundaries are clearly defined. If not effected areas to be put no hold prior to commencement of contract.		X
Construction	Clear and specific documentation not provided during Construction NOC submittal.	NOC obtained could be interpreted in more than one way in which material was approved to be installed by authority.	Negotiations undertaken with authority and agreed High to follow revised/updated specification in all future contracts.	High	Construction NOC submittals to be reviewed prior to submittial and once approved prior to commencement of installation.		X
Commercial	Nominated sub-contractor issued separate stand alone contract	Both contractors on site acting as main contractor with no coordination or regard for each other.	Due to both contracts let by client, PM used as liaison and coordinator between both parties.	High	Contents of contract needs to be followed by client. If two main contracts are let at the same time, each needs to reflect co-ordination and responsibility for the other.		X
Procurement							

Productivity Norms

17

17.1 INTRODUCTION

Productivity is critically important in the context of construction contracts both large and small. Contractors are typically paid for work completed in place that conforms to the terms of the contract. An efficient and effective labour force will achieve these objectives in time thus increasing the Contractor's revenue and reducing its costs.

Definition

The productivity is defined as the craft hours necessary to produce a unit of finished product, and it can be defined by any of the following equations:

Productivity = Output/Input

= Units/Work Hours

= Total Output/Total Work Hours.

17.2 FACTORS AFFECTING LABOUR PRODUCTIVITY

Labour productivity is affected by many factors and these are explained below:

Variable Location: Employees working at different height of the building will have different level of productive works. Also, availability of access and logistical supports are the other factors affecting the labour productivity.

Adverse Weather: Changes in weather like very hot, very cold, very windy, very wet, and very humid and snow will affect the labour productivity and due to the bad weather absentees of workers at site may increase. Hence the contractors will be achieving a different level of work productivity.

Work Load: Employees working with heavy work load or target work will create loss in quality of work and increase the need for re-working. Tiredness and speed cause inefficiency and the resulting poor quality.

Transportation: Employees late arrival to the site and early departure from site will affect the labour productivity, if the same amount of work has to be achieved in the shorter time. Again, quality suffers and re-working increases.

Shortages of Material, Tools and Equipment: Delay in procurement of materials and delivery to the site will create idle man-hours and eventually affects the labour productivity. If materials, tools or construction equipments are not available at the right location and time then the labour productivity will probably suffer as they may be unable to proceed with the works in an orderly and consistent manner. Similarly, if the wrong tools or improperly sized equipment is provided, this may also affect the labour productivity.

Field Organization and Management Factors: A result of poor Project Management is that the sequence of works is not properly planned/scheduled and the shortage or unavailability of critical construction equipments may lead to loss of labour productivity. For example, mobilizing the labours prior to having access to the site and electrical power supply.

Work Area Access Restrictions: If a work site is remote and difficult to get into or has inefficient or limited access and suffers from delay in issuance of permits, then the loss of productivity may occur due to the idle man-hours.

Stacking of Trades: To achieve good productivity, each crew member must have sufficient working space to perform his works without being interfered with by other members. When too many labourers are assigned to work in a limited work area, it is probable that interference may occur, thus affecting the labour productivity.

Poor Estimating: Loss of productivity may be the result of poor initial estimating by the Contractors. The Contractors may have simply miscalculated and/or failed to consider the various conditions under which the work will be executed.

17.3 HOW TO CONTROL THE LOSS OF LABOUR PRODUCTIVITY

A Contractor must control the loss of labour productivity to avoid the risks/costs associated with any loss in this respect. This may be done in a number of ways some of the most important of which are identified below.

Incentives: Labour efficiency and output can be improved by the introduction of incentive programs such as Open Book Management, The Green Stamp Program, Suggestion Program, Sharing Savings, Target Bonuses, Honoraria, Service Awards, Merit Raises, Cross Training, Special Training, Management by Walking Around, Certificates of Appreciation and Achievement, Certificates of Completion, Decals, Token Award, Employee or Crew of the Month, Problem-solving Teams and Team Builders to the Employees. All these incentive programs have been shown to increase labour performance and productivity, reduce waste, reduce absenteeism and improve the quality of works.

Insurance: Workmen's compensation and employee benefits insurance policies could be made available to all the employees and an insurance claim should include the remedy of an individual injured worker or of the family of one who dies as the result of an industrial accident.

Motivation: The motivation of the workforce to achieve higher production by introducing incentives such as bonuses, overtime and outstation allowances have been proven to encourage the people to work hard and thereby achieve more productivity.

Skilled Workers: Choosing properly skilled workers for the job. As people work at different rates of output, a person's experience and speed must be a factor when establishing productivity. For example, a junior member of the team might take two days to deliver a specific product whereas a more senior member who is having a unique complement of skills, knowledge, experience and competencies could do the same work in half the time.

Man Management: A structured man management program should be employed within engineering and construction phases and good management practice should be maintained with the employees through frequent visits to the work areas during which the managers should show sincere interest in the workforce and the works in order to create better relationships and get improved labour productivity.

Communication: A formal and informal structure of effective communication is absolutely essential in the work area, and with effective communication, all project participants can stimulate co-operation and productivity. However, as a result of the many people involved in a project, all with different personalities, cultures, nationalities and varying levels of understanding, the communication can be difficult and misunderstandings can arise. Company organizations can try to avoid that by giving guidelines for the effective communication of messages and by allowing people the freedom to organize some of the work and by treating people as important individuals.

Training: In-house or external training should be conducted for all labour categories. For example, when a company purchases new equipment, demonstration is to be given as how to use and maintain the same equipment as well as in the use and maintenance of any other power tools deployed for construction purposes.

Material Handling: Handling of material is a very important role in increasing labour productivity. Manual work should be avoided whenever equipment can be used to transfer the materials from one location to another location within the site. Company has to implement a proper efficient system in order to expedite the handling of materials on site to avoid waste of time, thereby increasing the labour productivity. Materials should be delivered to workforces in manageable packages so as to avoid loss of time in manipulating and re-handling the materials.

Health and Safety: Every measure should be taken to make the work place a hygienic one including proper sanitary facilities, proper drinking water facilities, proper dining and recreation room, good housekeeping, etc. Company organization should conduct safety induction courses for each employee and arrange regular safety meetings for all the workers and accordingly introduce strict compliance of using the right PPE (Personal Protective Equipment), proper sign boards, barricades and right tools or equipments to reduce the employee's exposure to hazards at work area.

Quality Control: Establish strict QA/QC procedures so that all employees understand the need to work accurately and precisely. Eliminating both poor quality workmanship and the consequent re-working to correct errors is a major contributory factor in improving labour productivity.

17.4 METHODS OF CALCULATING LOSS OF PRODUCTIVITY

The task of calculating and proving damages for loss of productivity represents one of the most difficult problems in construction claims. The Contractor bears the burden of proof in presenting a claim. The Contractor must demonstrate a cost impact through evidence that is persuasive enough to prove that the claimed costs were incurred as a result of extra work, adverse weather, etc. The most widely used methods by contractors to claim losses of productivity are detailed below:

Total Cost Method: In this method, the difference between the actual costs incurred and what had been estimated plus approved change orders are established. This method can be used for any category of direct costs. However, it is most often used to calculate labour related damages. In order to have acceptability of the total cost method, the following pre-requisites must be met:

- The nature of the particular loss must allow accurate calculation of the costs. Frequently, the type of loss makes it impossible or highly impractical to determine them with a reasonable degree of accuracy.
- The Contractor's bid or estimate was realistic and the total labour cost can be established.
- Its actual costs were reasonable and can be demonstrated.
- Contractor was not responsible for the added expenses, i.e., Contractor performance was reasonably efficient and the loss was, demonstrably, caused by external factors beyond Contractor's control.
- This method is often viewed with some scepticism and should be used only as a last resort when no other feasible method is available.

Table 1: Example for Total Cost Method

Description	Estimated Hrs	Actual Hrs	Variance Hrs	Hourly Rate (US$)
Activity 1	2000	2200	200	30
Approved change order	400	450	50	30
Total	**2400**	**2650**	**250**	**30**

Assume that all the pre-requisites are met in Table 1, then the total claim amount shall be 250 Hrs × US$ 30.00 = US$ 7500.00.

Modified Total Cost Method: This method is similar to the total cost method. It differs in the fact that a Contractor makes certain adjustments to its estimated cost by deducting the cost for inaccuracies or re-works for which the owner is not responsible. Thus, adding credibility to the claim.

Table 2: Example for Modified Total Cost Method

Description	Estimated Hrs	Actual Hrs	Variance Hrs	Hourly Rate (US$)
Activity 1	2000	2200	200	40
Approved change order	200	250	50	40
Re-works	0	-100	-100	40
Total	**2200**	**2350**	**150**	**40**

Assume that all the pre-requisites are met in Table 2, then the total claim amount shall be 150 Hrs × US$ 40.00 = US$ 6000.00.

Comparison of Productivity Levels: The best way to illustrate this method is through an example. Assume a Contractor had planned to perform all concrete work prior to the onset of winter, but due to an Owner causing delay, the Contractor was forced to perform part of the work during the winter. It is well-known and documented that concrete work performed during winter months is less productive than non-winter conditions. Actual job records of performance under winter and non-winter conditions would provide precise and accurate data to prove that a loss in productivity occurred. Labour time sheets and concrete pour records in Table 3 below would provide the necessary information.

Table 3: Data for Comparison of Productivity Levels

Description	Sept.-Nov.	Dec.-Mar.	April & May	Actual Total	Bid Total
Work Hours (WH)	3000	5000	1200	9200	7000
Quantity Concrete (CM)	1300	1400	600	3200	2900
WH/CM	**2.30**	**3.57**	**2**	**2.87**	**2.41**

As shown above, during the non-winter months (Sept-Nov. and April and May), the Contractor averaged 2.30 WH/CM for concrete work (3000 + 1200 divided by 1300 + 600). This compares with the 3.57 WH/CM that the Contractor experienced during the winter months of Dec.-Mar. This analysis shows the Contractor expended an additional 1.27 WH/CM (3.57 – 2.30) for work performed during the winter months. The additional cost resulting from the owner caused delay would be calculated as:

> Concrete poured Dec.-Mar. × Loss of Productivity @ 1.27 WH/CM = 1400 CM × 1.27 WH/CM = 1778 WH @ US$ 30.00 Per Hr = US$ 53340.00.

This method is also referred to as the cause and effect method. Obviously, proper documentation and substantiation are vital in accurately determining the amount of damages and also helping in proving that a loss was actually incurred, thus strengthening the Contractor's position and increasing the chances of recovery.

Measured Mile Method: This method is used on an extrapolation of actual work hours expended. It requires a period of unhindered time in which the labour expended reflects an efficient use for that type of work. Using this efficient time and the percentage of work accomplished and the related actual work hours, a theoretical estimate of the total efficient work hours required for completion of that type work can be derived, on that project.

Comparing this projected work hour estimate to the total actual work hours expended allows for a judgment as to the probable accuracy of total labour estimated and the efficient or inefficient use of those work hours.

A monthly summary of the actual per cent complete and the actual labour hours for each type of work to be investigated, as well as the labour budget hour estimate for the project, are the only data needed for the development of this analysis. The percentages are often available from the progress payment procedure and the budget estimate would be the Contractor's bid estimate.

Revenue per Work Hour Approach: Another method for identifying productivity trends is the revenue per work hour approach. This method compares the revenues earned for each labour work hour consumed during various time periods of the job. This approach is often used with total revenues but is most effective if labour revenues can be isolated. Caution is required, however, if significantly different work activities are performed that would inherently result in fluctuations of revenues per work hour.

Factor Approach: Many claims for lost productivity are computed on the so-called "factor approach". The factor approach is based on the application of lost efficiency "percentages" for various conditions (e.g. Stacking of trades, beneficial occupancy, etc.) to actual labour costs.

Numerous trade organizations have developed these productivity factors to quantify the economic impact on contractors.

The method in which the factors are applied is also very important. The application is different depending on whether the factors are applied prospectively or retrospectively. If one is prospectively pricing a change order where impacts are anticipated, the factor percentages should be added together and multiplied by the base (standard) work hours to determine unproductive work hours.

17.5 PRODUCTION RATES

17.5.1 Structural/Flooring /Masonry Works

Sl.No.	Description of Work	Gang Size	Production Rates	Remarks
	CONCRETING BY READY MIX			
1.	Blinding	1M + 4H	10.0 CuM	
2.	Footing/Pile Caps	1M + 4H	12.0 CuM	
3.	T. Beams/F. Beams	1M + 5H	1.0 CuM	
4.	Neck Columns			
5.	Ground Slab	3M + 6H	15.0 M^3	
6.	Suspended Slab Beam	3M + 6H	15.0 M^3	
	CONCRETING BY SITE MIX			
1.	Blinding	1M + 8H	1.0 M^3	
2.	Neck Columns		0.8 M^3	
3.	Superstructure Columns		1.0 M^3	
	STEEL REINFORCEMENT			
1.	Cut & Bend (18 – 25 Dia)	1 SF	50 Kg	
2.	Cut & Bend (8 – 16 Dia)	1 SF	40 Kg	
3.	Fixing (18 – 25 Dia)	1 SF	25 Kg	
4.	Fixing (8 – 16 Dia)	1 SF	20 Kg	
	BLOCKWORK			
1.	8 × 8 × 16	1M + 1H	1.2 SqM	
2.	4 × 8 × 16	1M + 1H	1.2 SqM	
3.	8″ Solid	1M + 1H	0.8 SqM	
	FINISHES			
1.	Internal Plaster	1M + 1H	1.50 SqM	
2.	External Plaster	1M + 1H	1.20 SqM	
3.	Plaster ARCH, DECO	1M + 1H	0.80 SqM	
4.	5 cm Floor Screed	1M + 1H	2.00 SqM	
5.	10 cm Roof Screed	1M + 1H	1.50 M^2	
6.	Mosaic Floor Tiles	1M + 1H	1.50 M^2	

(Contd.)

Sl.No.	Description of Work	Gang Size	Production Rates	Remarks
7.	15 × 15 Ceramic W. Tiles	1M + 1H	0.80 M^2	
8.	20 × 20 Ceramic W. Tiles	1M + 1H	1.00 M^2	
9.	Ceramic Floor Tiles	1M + 1H	1.00 M^2	
10.	Marble Flooring	1M + 1H	0.80 M^2	
11.	Marble Skirting	1M + 1H	2.00 M R	
12.	Tread, Riser	1M + 1H	5.00 M R	
13.	Hacking	1M + 1H	8.00 M^2	
14.	Spatter Dash	1 H	7.50 M^2	
	SUNDRIES			
1.	Polythene Laying	1H	8.00 M^2	
2.	Bitumen Paint	1H	7.00 M^2	
	SHUTTERING WORKS			
	SUB-STRUCTURE			
	BLINDING 2″			
1.	Make	1C + 1H	8.00 M R	
2.	Fix	1C + 1H	8.00 M R	
	FOOTINGS, PILECAPS			
1.	Make	1C + 1H	2.00 M^2	
2.	Fix	1C + 1H	1.50 M^2	
3.	De-shutter	1H	6.00 M^2	
	NECK COLUMNS			
1.	Make	1C + 1H	1.50 M^2	
2.	Fix	1C + 1H	1.20 M^2	
3.	De-shutter	1H	4.80 M^2	
	T. BEAMS, F. BEAMS, ETC.			
1.	Make	1C + 1H	1.20 M^2	
2.	Fix	1C + 1H	1.00 M^2	
3.	De-shutter	1H	4.00 M^2	
	SUPERSTRUCTURE			
	COLUMNS			
1.	Make	1C + 1H	1.50 M^2	
2.	Fix	1C + 1H	1.00 M^2	
3.	De-shutter	1H	4.00 M^2	
	WALLS			
1.	Make	1C + 1H	1.20 M^2	
2.	Fix	1C + 1H	0.80 M^2	
3.	De-Shutter	1H	3.20 M^2	

(Contd.)

Sl.No.	Description of Work	Gang Size	Production Rates	Remarks
	STAIRCASES			
1.	Make	1C + 1H	0.80 M^2	
2.	Fix	1C + 1H	0.50 M^2	
3.	De-shutter	1H	4.00 M^2	
	DROP BEAMS			
1.	Make	1C + 1H	1.00 M^2	
2.	Fix	1C + 1H	0.80 M^2	
3.	De-shutter	1H	3.20 M^2	
	INVERTED BEAMS			
1.	Make	1C + 1H	1.50 M^2	
2.	Fix	1C + 1H	1.00 M^2	
3.	De-shutter	1H	4.00 M^2	
	SUSPENDED SLABS			
1.	Fix	1C + 1H	1.20 M^2	
2.	De-shutter	1H	5.00 M^2	
	DECK FORMWORK			
1.	Fix	1C + 1H	1.50 M^2	
2.	De-shutter	1H	6.00 M^2	
	SUNSHADES			
1.	Fix	1C + 1H	0.70 M^2	
2.	De-shutter	1H	3.00 M^2	
	PARAPETS			
1.	Make	1C + 1H	1.20 M^2	
2.	Fix	1C + 1H	1.00 M^2	
3.	De-shutter	1H	4.00 M^2	
	LINTELS			
1.	Fix	1C + 1H	0.50 M^2	
2.	De-shutter	1H	2.00 M^2	

M-Mason, H-Helper, SF-Steel Fixer,

17.5.2 Piling Work

Sl.No.	Description of Work	Gang Size	Production Rates	Remarks
1.	Piles with 1.5, 2 & 2.5 Mt dia.	2 Rigs	12-14 nos./Day	Production will vary with length and dia of piles
2.	Concrete to Pile Caps by Pump	6 Mason + 18 Helper + 1 Carpenter + 1 Steel Fixer	180 Cum/Day	

17.5.3 Kerbing/Block Paving Works

Sl.No.	Description of Work	Gang Size	Production Rates	Remarks
1.	Kerbstone (Without PCC)	1 Mason + 1 Helper	15 LM/Day	
2.	Interlock Paving on Prepared Sub-Base	1 Mason + 2 Helper	40 Sqm/Day	
3.	Screed Works incld. Preparation 50mm thick.	1 Mason + 1 Helper	15 Sqm/Day	

17.5.4 Manhole/Drainage

Sl.No.	Description of Work	Gang Size	Production Rates	Remarks
1.	Excavation for Drains/Manholes (Sand)	1 Helper	5 Cum/Day	
2.	Backfill to Drains/Manholes	1 Helper	10 Cum/Day	
3.	Block Works to Manholes (Medium)	2 Mason + 1 Helper	4 nos	
4.	Plaster to Manholes(Medium Size)	2 Mason + 1 Helper	4 nos	
5.	Benching to Manholes	2 Mason + 1 Helper	8 nos	

17.5.5 Painting Preparatory Work

Sl.No.	Description Preparation	Slow	Ave.	Fast	Unit m^2/hr
1.	Prepare Walls		14.2		m^2/hr
2.	Prepare Doors		12.5		m^2/hr
3.	Prepare Door Frames		25		m^2/hr
4.	Burn Off/Heat Strip Paintwork		1.1		m^2/hr
5.	Internal Timber, 1 coat primer before fixing, generally		6.7		m^2/hr

17.5.6 Earth Work

Sl.No.	Description	Slow	Ave.	Fast	Unit
1.	Excavate Spoil Heaps to Transport, 0.6 m^3 bucket, Sand/Soil	14.5	20.0	25.6	m^3/hr
2.	Excavate Spoil Heaps to Transport, 0.6 m^3 bucket, Gravel Beds	15.2	20.4	25.6	m^3/hr
3.	Excavate Spoil Heaps to Transport, 0.6 m^3 bucket, Clay/Chalk	12.3	18.5	23.2	m^3/hr
4.	Excavate Spoil Heaps to Transport, 0.6 m^3 bucket, Boulder Clay	11.2	16.9	21.3	m^3/hr
5.	Excavate Spoil Heaps to Transport, 1.1 m^3 bucket, Sand/Soil	25.4	30.3	35.7	m^3/hr
6.	Excavate Spoil Heaps to Transport, 1.1 m^3 bucket, Gravel Beds	25.6	31.3	37.0	m^3/hr
7.	Excavate Spoil Heaps to Transport, 1.1 m^3 bucket, Clay/Chalk	22.5	27.8	33.3	m^3/hr
8.	Excavate Spoil Heaps to Transport, 1.1 m^3 bucket, Boulder Clay	18.9	24.4	30.3	m^3/hr
9.	Load Spoil to Barge, capacity 2,000 m^3	-	8.0	-	hrs
10.	Load Spoil to Barge, capacity 1,500 m^3	-	6.5	-	hrs
11.	Load Spoil to Barge, capacity 1,000 m^3	-	5.5	-	hrs
12.	Spoil conveyor, 600 mm belt, 150 m/min	-	260.0	-	m^3/hr

17.5.7 Spread and Level

Sl.No.	Description	Slow	Ave.	Fast	Unit
1.	Crawler Shovel, 0.8 m^3 bucket, Sand/Soil, pushed 5-50 m to stockpile	13.9	20.4	25.0	m^3/hr
2.	Crawler Shovel, 0.8 m^3 bucket, Sand/Soil, pushed 50-120 m to stockpile	7.6	9.5	12.6	m^3/hr
3.	Crawler Shovel, 0.8 m^3 bucket, Gravel, pushed 5-50 m to stockpile	14.2	20.4	25.6	m^3/hr
4.	Crawler Shovel, 0.8 m^3 bucket, Gravel, pushed 50-120 m to stockpile	7.6	10.2	12.8	m^3/hr
5.	Crawler Shovel, 0.8 m^3 bucket, Clay/Chalk, pushed 5-50 m to stockpile	12.7	18.4	23.2	m^3/hr
6.	Crawler Shovel, 0.8 m^3 bucket, Clay/Chalk, pushed 50-120 m to stockpile	6.9	8.9	11.6	m^3/hr
7.	Crawler Shovel, 0.8 m3 bucket, Boulder Clay, pushed 5-50 m to stockpile	11.6	16.9	21.3	m^3/hr
8.	Crawler Shovel, 0.8 m^3 bucket, Boulder Clay, pushed 50-120 m to stockpile	6.3	8.2	10.4	m^3/hr
9.	Crawler Shovel, 1.2 m^3 bucket, Sand/Soil, pushed 5-50 m to stockpile	23.8	28.5	35.7	m^3/hr
10.	Crawler Shovel, 1.2 m^3 bucket, Sand/Soil, pushed 50-120 m to stockpile	16.7	18.5	20.4	m^3/hr
11.	Crawler Shovel, 1.2 m^3 bucket, Gravel, pushed 5-50 m to stockpile	25.0	32.0	37.0	m^3/hr
12.	Crawler Shovel, 1.2 m^3 bucket, Gravel, pushed 50-120 m to stockpile	17.2	19.3	21.2	m^3/hr
13.	Crawler Shovel, 1.2 m^3 bucket, Clay/Chalk, pushed 5-50 m to stockpile	21.7	27.5	33.3	m^3/hr
14.	Crawler Shovel, 1.2 m^3 bucket, Clay/Chalk, pushed 50-120 m to stockpile	15.1	16.9	18.8	m^3/hr
15.	Crawler Shovel, 1.2 m^3 bucket, Boulder Clay, pushed 5-50 m to stockpile	19.6	24.5	30.3	m^3/hr
16.	Crawler Shovel, 1.2 m^3 bucket, Boulder Clay, pushed 50-120 m to stockpile	13.7	15.9	17.5	m^3/hr
17.	Crawler Shovel, 0.6 m^3 bucket, 50-200 m^2, Sand/Soil	18.6	28.5	38.5	m^3/hr
18.	Crawler Shovel, 0.6 m^3 bucket, over 200 m^2, Sand/Soil	24.4	37.2	50.0	m^3/hr
19.	Crawler Shovel, 0.6 m^3 bucket, 50-200 m^2, Gravel	18.9	28.6	38.4	m^3/hr
20.	Crawler Shovel, 0.6 m^3 bucket, over 200 m^2, Gravel	24.2	37.2	50.0	m^3/hr
21.	Crawler Shovel, 0.6 m^3 bucket, 50-200 m^2, Hardcore	15.8	23.5	31.2	m^3/hr
22.	Crawler Shovel, 0.6 m^3 bucket, over 200 m^2, Hardcore	19.2	29.6	40.0	m^3/hr
23.	Crawler Shovel, 0.6 m^3 bucket, 50-200 m^2, Boulder Clay	17.2	26.4	35.7	m^3/hr
24.	Crawler Shovel, 0.6 m^3 bucket, over 200 m^2, Boulder Clay	22.2	33.8	45.4	m^3/hr
25.	Crawler Shovel, 1.2 m^3 bucket, 50-200 m^2, Sand/Soil	43.5	48.0	52.6	m^3/hr
26.	Crawler Shovel, 1.2 m^3 bucket, over 200 m^2, Sand/Soil	55.5	61.1	66.7	m^3/hr
27.	Crawler Shovel, 1.2 m^3 bucket, 50-200 m^2, Gravel	43.8	48.3	52.9	m^3/hr
28.	Crawler Shovel, 1.2 m^3 bucket, over 200 m^2, Gravel	55.5	61.1	66.7	m^3/hr
29.	Crawler Shovel, 1.2 m^3 bucket, 50-200 m^2, Hardcore	37.1	40.3	43.5	m^3/hr
30.	Crawler Shovel, 1.2 m^3 bucket, over 200 m^2, Hardcore	47.6	51.6	55.6	m^3/hr
31.	Crawler Shovel, 1.2 m^3 bucket, 50-200 m^2, Boulder Clay	43.8	45.7	47.6	m^3/hr
32.	Crawler Shovel, 1.2 m^3 bucket, over 200 m^2, Boulder Clay	55.6	59.1	62.5	m^3/hr

17.5.8 Fencing Work

Sl.No.	Description	Slow	Ave.	Fast	Unit
1.	Site Hoarding, timber posts, plywood nailed to horizontal rails	1.0	1.2	-	m/hr
2.	Post Erection, Timber/Metal, dig, erect, fix	3.3	4.5	-	m/hr
3.	Post Erection, Concrete, dig, erect, fix	3.2	4.0	-	m/hr
4.	Fence Erection, Chain-link, posts at 1.5 m	-	4.2	-	m/hr
5.	Fence Erection, Chain-link, posts at 2.0 m	-	4.4	-	m/hr

17.5.9 Power Supply

Sl.No.	Description	Slow	Ave.	Fast	Unit
1.	AC Install 2 no Service transformers, 6 men	-	12		Days
2.	AC Install 2 no Switchgear, 7 men	-	12		Days
3.	AC Install Associated Trays and ladders, 3 men	11.0	5.0		Days
4.	AC Cable Terminations in Tx and SWG Rooms, 3 men	12.0	6.0		Days
5.	DC Install Insulated Flooring in DC Room, 1 man	-	5.0		Days
6.	DC Install 1 set Rectifier Transformer and Rectifier, 7 men	-	1.0		Days
7.	DC Install Switchgear, 7 men	-	10.0		Days
8.	DC Primary Cable Terminations and Bus duct, 18 men	12.0	9		Days
9.	DC Secondary Cable Terminations and Connections, 9 men	12.0	6		Days
10.	Trackside Cabling 33 kV/Pilot Cables, 10 men	2100	-		M run/Day
11.	Trackside Cabling Terminations, 6 men	-	1.0		Days

17.5.10 Lift Installation

Sl.No.	Description	Slow	Ave.	Fast	Unit
1.	Hydraulic Lift, Install 2 to 3 storeys	-	3.0	-	Wks/Flr
2.	Hydraulic Lift, Install 4 storeys and above	-	2.0	-	Wks/Flr
3.	Hydraulic Lift, Testing allow 2 wks plus	-	1.0	-	Day/Flr
4.	Standard Lift, Manufacture, test and deliver	-	12.0	-	Wks
5.	Non-Standard Lift, Manufacture, test and deliver	75	65.0	52	Wks

Progress Reports: Content and Template

18

18.1 CONTRACTOR WEEKLY REPORT

Content Outline

1. Project Particulars
2. Overall Progress Status:
   - 2.1 Works (Area/Sector for Villas, Tower/Towers each)—Civil/MEP/Others
   - 2.2 Rate of Progress Analysis (Area/Sector for Villas, Tower/Towers each)—Civil/MEP/Others
   - 2.3 Mitigation Measures (Area/Sector for Villas, Tower/Towers each)—Civil/MEP/Others
   - 2.4 Mock-ups
3. Overdue/Critical Issues:
   - 3.1 Consultant
   - 3.2 Client
   - 3.3 3rd Party
4. 4 Weeks Look-ahead Program progress update
5. Construction N.O.C's Status
6. Statutory Authority Submission of shop drawings DEWA/Civil Defence/Others
7. Provisional Sums and Prime Cost Register
8. Tracking Logs:
   - 8.1 Materials (Arch/Structural/MEP/Others)
   - 8.2 Shop Drawings (Arch/Structural/MEP/Others)
   - 8.3 RFI
   - 8.4 NCR
   - 8.5 Method Statements (Arch/Structural/MEP/Others)
   - 8.6 Long Lead Items Procurement Status (Civil/MEP/Others)
   - 8.7 Sub-contractor Procurement schedule
9. Manpower Status (Planned vs. Actual for Area/each Tower):
   - 9.1 Civil (Discipline identified)

9.2 MEP (Discipline identified)
9.3 Others (Discipline identified)

10. Plant and Machinery (Planned vs. Actual) Status
11. Safety Summary—Health Safety and Environment (HSE):
    11.1 Housekeeping
    11.2 Tool box Talks
    11.3 LTA Log
    11.4 Near misses
12. Quality Assurance:
    12.1 Mock-ups
    12.2 Inspection of Installation
    12.3 Material Inspections
    12.4 Testing and Commissioning Inspections
    12.5 Work Notifications

18.2 CONTRACTOR MONTHLY REPORT

Content Outline

1. Project Data
2. Executive Summary (for each area/Tower):
    2.1 Planned vs. Actual progress of works during the month
    2.2 Rate of Progress Analysis
    2.3 Sufficiency of Recovery/Mitigation measures adopted
    2.4 Mock-up
3. Overdue/Critical Issues:
    3.1 Consultant
    3.2 Client
    3.3 3rd Party
4. Clause 14 Program progress updates (Civil/MEP and Others):
    4.1 Recovery Program progress updates (Civil/MEP and Others)
    4.2 Next 4 weeks Look-ahead Program
5. Plan vs. Actual Progress Indicators (S-curves):
    5.1 Overall
    5.2 Structure (for each area/Tower)
    5.3 MEP (for each area/Tower)
    5.4 Finishing-Block works, Plaster, False ceiling, Painting, Tiling, Aluminium cladding, Glazing works, Building envelope (as applicable or as required for each area/Tower)

6. Progress update on Provisional sums and Prime Cost items
7. Tracking Logs:
   - 7.1 Summary of Material Tracking Log and Long-lead Items
   - 7.2 Summary of Shop drawings Submittal, Approval and Tracking Log
   - 7.3 Provisional Sum/Prime Cost Item Tracking Log
   - 7.4 Sub-contractor Procurement Tracking Log
   - 7.5 Summary RFI Tracking Log
   - 7.6 Summary of QA/QC Inspection Log
   - 7.7 Summary of NCR Log
   - 7.8 Method Statement Log
   - 7.9 Engineer's Instruction Tracking Log
   - 7.10 Statutory Authority Submissions/Approvals
   - 7.11 Analysis for variance in submissions for items 7.1 to 7.4 and 7.8, and recovery measures adopted by the contractor for each category/discipline.
8. Financial Summary (Civil, MEP and Others):
   - 8.1 Planned vs. Actual Cash Flow
   - 8.2 Analysis for variance in Cash flow, recovery measures
   - 8.3 Payment status
   - 8.4 Variations
9. Manpower Summary (Civil, MEP and Others):
   - 9.1 Planned vs. Actual
   - 9.2 Analysis for variance, recovery measures
   - 9.3 Additional resource deployment plan
10. Equipment Report Civil, MEP and Others:
    - 10.1 Planned vs. Actual
    - 10.2 Analysis for variance, recovery measures
11. Safety Summary
12. Quality Assurance
13. Progress Photos
14. Attachments (soft copy):
    - 14.1 CL 14 Program update
    - 14.2 4 weeks look-ahead program
    - 14.3 Tracking Logs
    - 14.4 Progress Photographs

18.3 CONSULTANT MONTHLY DESIGN PROGRESS REPORT

Content Outline

1. Project Data
2. Scope of Work
3. Executive Summary:
   - 3.1 Overall design progress of works and respective breakdowns of deliverables by sector/area/tower.
   - 3.2 Overview on the planned vs. actual progress on interior design (if under consultant's scope).
   - 3.3 Overview on the planned vs. actual progress on integration of main design and interior design.
   - 3.4 Overview on the planned vs. actual progress on finalizing the design for PC/PS items.
   - 3.5 Overview on the procurement of sub-consultants and deliverables.
   - 3.6 Overdue/critical issues/identified potential risk from the following sources:
     - Consultant/sub-consultant
     - Dubai Properties
     - 3rd Party
4. Overview on Financial Status of the Project:
   - 4.1 Overview on the planned vs. actual budget analysis for the project.
   - 4.2 Cash flow (monthly and cumulative) histogram covering consultant and contractor.
   - 4.3 Payment status (for contractors, sub-contractors and sub-consultants).
5. Variations
6. Integrated Baseline Program:
   - 6.1 Project progress update
   - 6.2 Recovery program progress update (if applicable)
7. Tracking Logs:
   - 7.1 Drawing Submittal Tracking Log
   - 7.2 Provisional Sum/Prime Cost Items Tracking Log
8. Status of statutory authorities submissions and approvals (e.g. Zoning Authority, DEWA, Civil Defence) for design NOCs.
9. Soft Copy Attachments:
   - 9.1 Baseline Program update
   - 9.2 Tracking Logs (see section 7)

Notes:

(a) Monthly progress reports to be submitted to the Project Manager by the 7th working day of the next month.

(b) For any part of the executive summary which shows delay, the Consultant shall specify recovery measures planned to mitigate the situation.

18.4 CONSULTANT MONTHLY SUPERVISION PROGRESS REPORT

Content Outline

1. Project Data
2. Scope of Work
3. Executive Summary:
   - 3.1 Overall construction progress of works and respective breakdowns by sector/area/tower.
   - 3.2 Overview on the contractor's planned vs. actual progress on submittals (materials, shop drawings, method statements).
   - 3.3 Overview on the planned vs. actual progress on material procurement (ordering/manufacturing/inspection/delivery of long lead items).
   - 3.4 Overview on the statutory authority submissions and approvals.
   - 3.5 Overview on the preparation and submission of testing and commissioning method statements, O&M manuals, training, as built drawings (if applicable).
   - 3.6 Overview on the planned vs. actual progress on resolution of PC/PS items.
   - 3.7 Overview on the procurement of sub-contractors.
   - 3.8 Overview on the planned vs. actual manpower resources: indirect, supervision, direct resources on the job (by discipline).
   - 3.9 Overview on the planned vs. actual equipment on site.
   - 3.10 Overdue/Critical Issues/Identified Potential Risk from the following sources:
     - Contractor/sub-contractor
     - Consultant
     - Dubai Properties
     - 3rd Party
4. Overview on Financial Status of the Project:
   - 4.1 Overview on the planned vs. actual budget analysis for the project.
   - 4.2 Cash flow (monthly and cumulative) histogram covering consultant and contractor.
   - 4.3 Payment status (for contractors, sub-contractors and sub-consultants)
5. Integrated Clause 14 Program:
   - 5.1 Project progress update in P3 (minimum) hard copy format
   - 5.2 Recovery program progress update
6. Contractor's planned vs. actual progress indicators (S-curves) extracted from the P3 program of works, including:
   - 6.1 Overall
   - 6.2 Structure
   - 6.3 MEP
   - 6.4 Finishing (block work, plaster, false ceiling, tiling, aluminium and glazing, wardrobes and vanity, kitchen cabinets, painting, aluminium cladding as applicable).

7. Contractor/Sub-contractor Tracking Logs:
   7.1 Material Submittal and Procurement Tracking Log
   7.2 Drawing Submittal Tracking Log
   7.3 Provisional Sum/Prime Cost Items Tracking Log
   7.4 RFI Tracking Log
   7.5 Method Statement Tracking Log
8. Variations
9. Engineer's Instruction Tracking Log
10. Overview on compliance to Quality Control requirements:
    10.1 Inspection test plan
    10.2 Close-out of NCR's
    10.3 Mock-up Approvals
    10.4 Factory Inspections
    10.5 Material Inspections at site
    10.6 Site Inspections
11. Overview on compliance to HSE requirements:
    11.1 Near Misses
    11.2 Accidents
    11.3 Cranes and hoists
    11.4 Housekeeping at site
12. Latest Progress Photos
13. Soft Copy Attachments:
    13.1 Clause 14 Program update
    13.2 Two to four week look ahead program
    13.3 Tracking Logs (see section 7)

Notes:

(a) Monthly progress reports to be submitted to the Project Manager by the 7th working day of the next month.

(b) The term "Contractor" refers to the contractor and his sub-contractors.

(c) For any part of the executive summary which shows delay, the consultant shall specify recovery measures planned to mitigate the situation.

"Performance reporting involves the development and dissemination of documents and exhibits that show the status of the project at given point in time."

18.5 TEMPLATES

18.5.1 Daily Report

[PROJECT NAME]
DAILY CONSTRUCTION REPORT

Date: ____________________

Day

S	S	M	T	W	TH	F

Contractor:
Contract:

Report No.

Temp. °C

0 - 30	30 - 40	40 - 50	50 up

Weather

Bright Sun	Clear	Overcast	Rain	Dust

Sea

Still	Moder	High

Humidity

Dry	Moder	Humid

Wind

Dry	Moder	Humid

Machinery Used

	Compressor(s)	Hoist(s)	Trailer(s)	Vibrator(s)	Welding Machine(s)	Traffic Car(s)	Pickup(s)
Size No. On Site Down Time							
	Dumper(s)	Level(s)	Theodoliter(s)	Compressor(s)	Grader(s)	Roller(s)	Concrete Pump
Size No. On Site Down Time							
	Bending Machine(s)	Wood/Marble Brick Cutter(s)	Welding Machine(s)	Bobcat(s)	Generator(s)		
Size No. On Site Down Time							
	Tower Crane(s)	Crane(s)	Backhoe(s)	Backhoe(s) with Jack	Transmit Concrete Mixer	Dump Truck(s)	6-Wheel Truck(s)
Size No. On Site Down Time							

Material & Equipments Delivered to Site

Description	Quantity	Units	Origin/Manufacturer

Manpower available at site

Occupation	Staff		Occupation	Labour		Daily Total	Cum Total
	Contract	Actual		Skilled	Unskilled		
Project Manager Construction Manager Planning Engineer Civil Engineer Architect Mechanical Engineer (Plum.) Mechanical Engineer (HVAC) Electrical Engineer Marine Engineer Safety Officer Q.C. Officer Secretary / Clerk General Foreman Civil Foreman Electrical Foreman Surveyors Assistant Surveyor Drivers Machine Operators Others			Carpenter Rebar Fixers Structural Steel Welder Tiler Joiner Marble Fixer Ceramic Mosaic Store Precast Aluminum Painter False Celling Glazing Plasterer(s) Plumber HVAC Electrician Labours				
Total			Total				

Work-in-Progress

Activity #	Description and Location of Work-in-Progress	Date		% Comp.	Remarks
		Started	Actual/Expected		

Remarks

DATE:
DISTRIBUTION

CC: Client ☐ PM ☐ Consultant ☐

18.5.2 Executive Snapshot

Project | Report Issue
Project Manager: | Previous Issue

Progress this week

Task	Due Date	Target Date

Next Week Actions

Task	Due Date

Commercial Summary **AEDM's**

Baseline project value Approved Valuations Total Pending Variations	
Total Forecast Cost	

Program Summary

Baseline Progress to Date	%
Actual Progress to Date	%
Variance	#VALUE!
Reason(s) for variance	

Key Milestones

Milestone	Baseline	Actual	Variance

Page 1

Top 5 Risks

Description	Ranking	Mitigating Actions	Trend

Issues and Decisions

Issues / Decision to be taken	Action Recommended	Owner	Required

18.5.3 Monthly Progress Report (Program Analysis)

CLIENT PROJECT LOGO	**Project Name** MONTHLY PROGRESS REPORT **PROGRAM ANALYSIS**	CONSULTANT LOGO CONTRACTOR LOGO

PHYSICAL PROGRESS		
Planned	%	30.00%
Actual	%	25.00%
Variance	%	5.00%

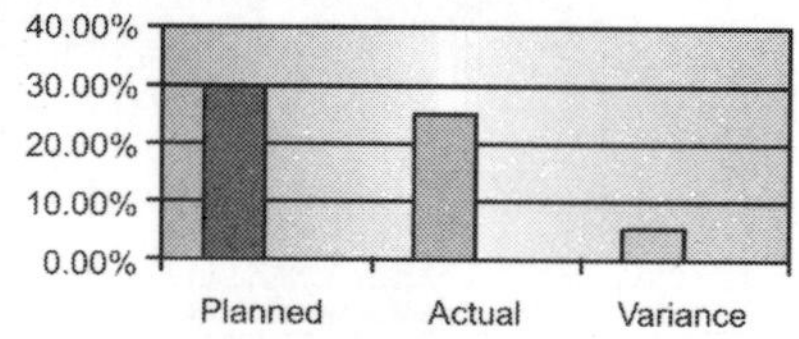

FINANCIAL STATUS		
Budgeted Cost	AED	925,475,500
Planned to date	AED	235,656,987
Work Performed to date	AED	226,678,200
Received to date	AED	225,690,332
Planned	%	25.46%
Actual	%	24.49%
Variance	%	0.97%

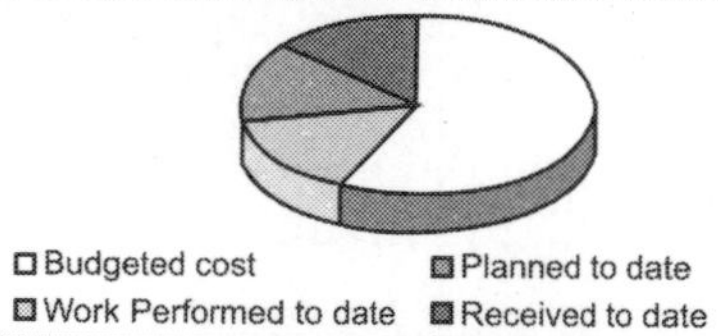

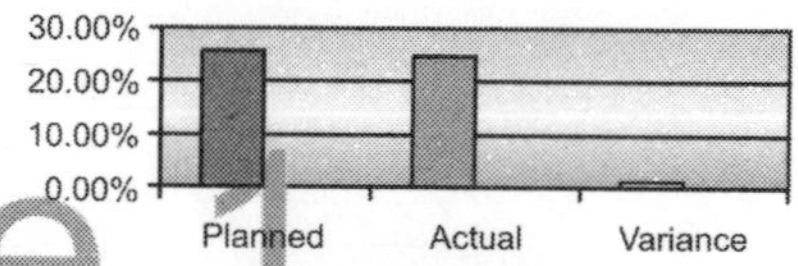

Page 1

TIME		Days	%
Contract Duration	Days	560	100%
Elapsed Duration	Days	230	41%
Remaining Duration	Days	330	59%

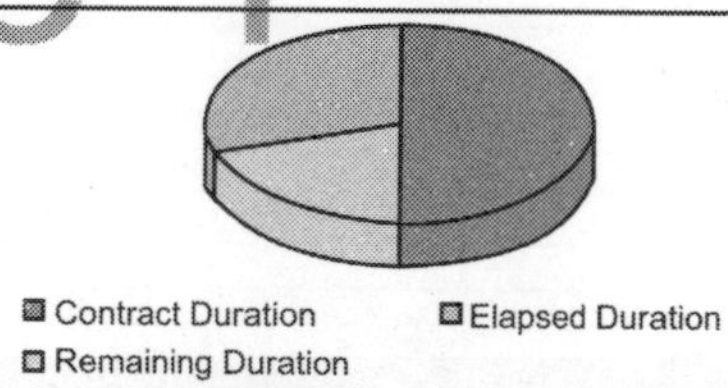

RESOURCES		
Manpower		
Planned	Man-days	980
Actual	Man-days	786
Variance	Man-days	194

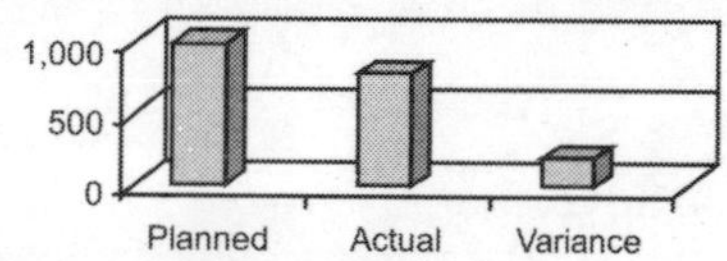

Plant and Equipments		
Planned	Machine Days	4,543
Actual	Machine Days	4,356
Variance	Machine Days	187

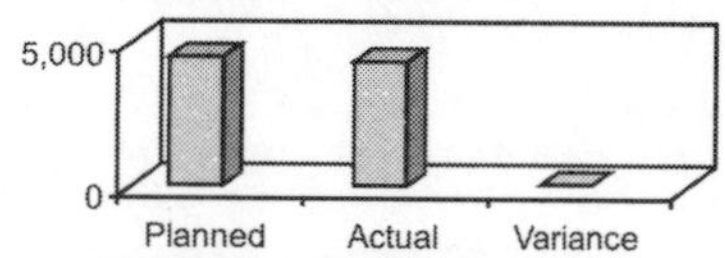

FLOAT ANALYSIS		
Current	Days	-89
Previous	Days	-60
Variance	Days	-29

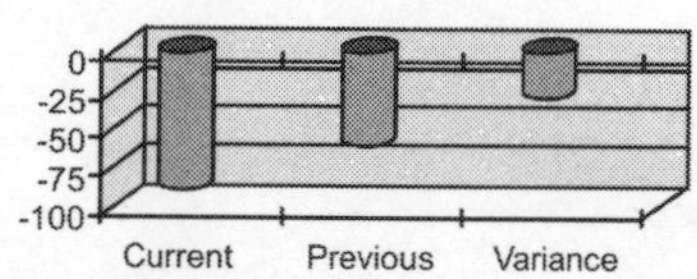

18.5.4 Weekly Flash Report

Project Name

Report Period Ending:

Project Time

PROJECT TIME STATUS IN %

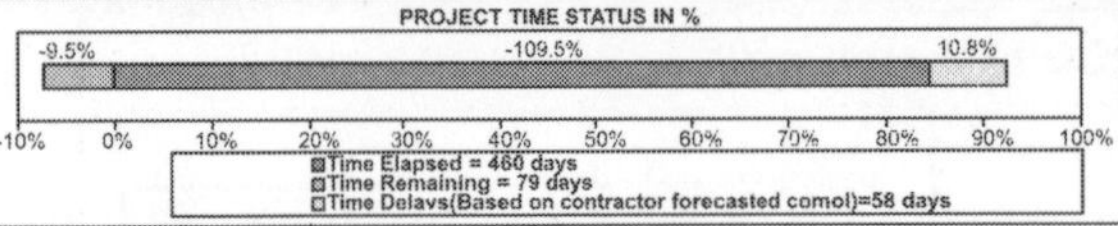

Start Date		Completion Date					
Start Date	Actual Const Start Date	Original Duration	Centrata of Compl	Forecasted Date Compl (Based on Program Update)			
19 Sep-06	16 Jan-07	420.00	12 Nov-07	17 Sep-08			

BUDGET STATUS

Description	Certified to Date	Budget (Dhs)
Contractor Lump Sum Work (Inc Adv Payment)	77,987,175.05	160,070,644.00
Variation and Additional Works	3,300,529.45	25,133,892.00
Claims for EOT (Estimated Final Max)	0.00	10,000,000.00
Total	81,287,704.50	195,204,536.00
Ramaining Budget		113,916,831.50

OVERALL COMPLETED WORK STATUS

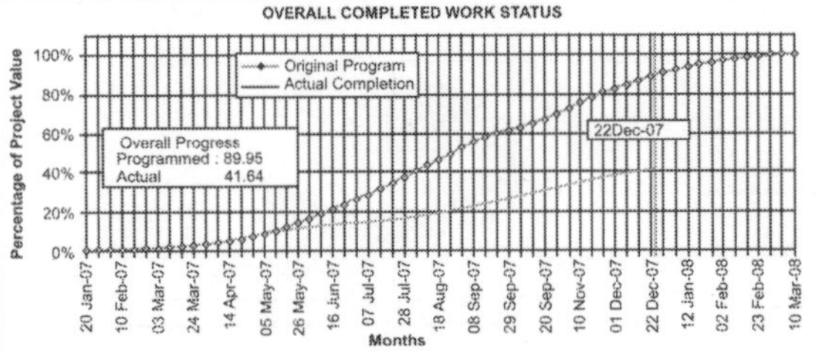

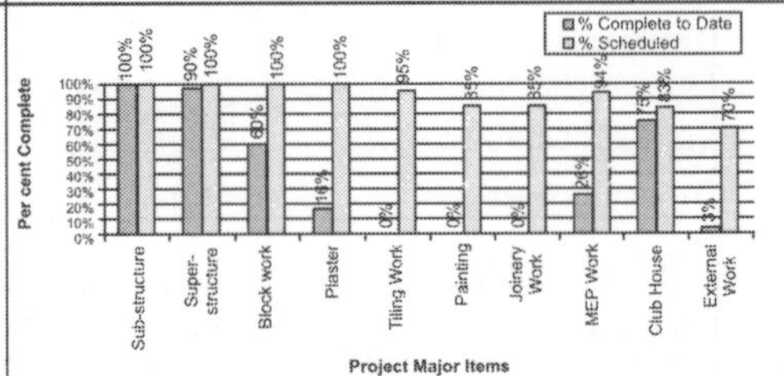

Design Status		**Action Log**	**Critical Issues**	**Action Log**
Construction Status			**Client**	**Action Log**
Critical	For follow up		For information	

External Plaster Preparation for Villa A 33, 34

Initial Coating for External Wall for Villa B 19, 20

Steel Fixing at Roof Slab for Villas C 81, 82, 83, 84

Blockworks on Progress in Ground Floor for Clubhouse

Control Forms

19

19.1 MATRIX FOR SITE ADMINISTRATION AND COMMUNICATION

P–Perform and Distribute Copies (As Noted) CC–All Information (Copy)

R–Review and Initial (Copy) D–Advise (Copy)

A–Approval (Original) TS–Transmittal Sheet Only (Copy)

Sl. No.	Issues	Contractor	Consultant	The Project Manager	The Client
1.	Notice to Commence	–	CC	P	CC
2.	Performance bond	P	–	R	A
3.	Advance payment guarantees	P	–	R	A
4.	Insurance Certificates	P	–	R	A
5.	Building Permits	P	D	R	CC
6.	Approval of sources and manufacturers not in specifications	P	R1	R2/A	–
7.	Approval of sources and manufacturers listed in the specifications	P	A	CC	–
8.	Approval of all sub-contractors	P	R1	R2/A	–
9.	Key site personnel	P	D	R/A	–
10.	Contractor's	P	D	R/A	–
11.	Schedule of Values and Cost Loaded Schedule	P	D	R/A	–
12.	Updated schedule without extension of time	P	D	A	–
13.	Payment Certificates	P	R1	R2	A
14.	Request for interpretation/clarification of contract documents that doesn't entail any change in cost or time (contractually)	P	R	A	CC
15.	Request for information of contract documents that doesn't entail any change in cost or time (technically) (RFI)	P	R/D	CC/A	CC
16.	Request for Inspection and Approval (R.F.I.A.)	P	A	CC	CC
17.	Request for Inspection and Approval—Demolition (R.F.I.A.D.)	P	R/D	CC/A	CC

(Contd.)

Sl. No.	Issues	Contractor	Consultant	The Project Manager	The Client
18.	Request for Proposal RFP	R	R	P	P/A
19.	Variations to the contract (V.O.)	–	R1	P/R2	A
20.	Site Work Instruction (S.W.I.) may entail additional cost of time	–	R1	P/R2	A
21.	Suspensions of work	–	R	P/A	CC
22.	Extension of time	–	D	P/R	A
23.	Any deviation from the contract documents, in respect of materials, that doesn't entail any change in cost or time	P	R1	A	–
24.	Any deviation from the contract documents that entails change in cost or time	P	R1	R2	A
25.	All corresp. which affects the terms and conditions of the contract	P	D	R/A	–
26.	Coordination among contractors	P	R	A/CC	–
27.	Submit all log (E1) and Procurement, shipment, and delivery schedule (E2)	P	D	A/CC	–
28.	On-site and off-site logistics	P	R	A/CC	–
29.	Safety plan and procedures	P	R	A	CC
30.	Exec. of the work in accordance with the contract drawings and spaces	P	A	A	CC
31.	Quality assurance and control	P	A	D	CC
32.	Submittals—shop drawings	P	A	TS	CC
33.	Submittals—finishes samples and mockups	P	R1	R2	CC
34.	Submittals—other samples and mockups	P	A	CC	A
35.	As-built drawings	P	A	CC	TS
36.	Supervision and inspection	–	P/A	CC	TS
37.	Non-compliance (Or Remedial Action) Notice	CC	P/A	CC	TS
38.	Surveys, levels and setting out	P	A	CC	CC
39.	Testing and commissioning	P	A	D	CC
40.	Maintenance manuals and certificates	P	R1	R2	A
41.	Guarantees and Warranties	P	R1	R2	A
42.	Substantial Completion	P	R1	R2	A

19.2 CONSTRUCTION INITIATION CHECKLIST

Project Name | Consultant: | Date:
Project No: | Sub-consultant:
Project Manager: | Contractor:
External Project Manager: | Sub-contractor:

Sl.No.	Requirements	Req'd pre-kick-up	Responsibility	Due Date	Submitted Date	Approved Y/N	Remarks
1.	Drawings Issued for Construction	☑					
2.	Specifications Issued for Construction	☑					
3.	BOQ Issued for Construction	☑					
4.	Insurance Policy Documents (as per contract)	☑					
5.	Performance Bond	☑					
6.	Advance Payment Bank Guarantee	☑					
7.	Site Organization chart and CV's						
8.	Excavation/Hoarding Permit						
9.	Building Permit						
10.	Design NOC from Authorities						
11.	Copy of Trade Licences						
12.	Site set-up and hoarding proposal						
13.	Sign board proposal						
14.	Site facilities and temporary services proposal						
15.	Condition survey of existing roads						
16.	Site level survey						
17.	Contractor's clause 14 program of works						
18.	Resource Histogram						
19.	Cash form estimate						
20.	Cost Breakdown						
21.	Outstanding information						
22.	HSE Plan						
23.	Inspection and test plan						
24.	QA/QC Plan						
25.	List of proposed suppliers and Sub-contractors						
26.	Daily, Weekly and Monthly report formals						
27.	Provisional sum items						
28.	Overall method statement						

19.3 PAYMENT CERTIFICATE

[PROJECT NAME]

Payment Certificate

☐ Advance Pay:	Bond #	Expiration:
☐ Interim Pay:		
☐ Exchange of Retention:	Bond #	Expiration:
☐ Final Pay and Release of Retention:		
☐ Single and Final Pay Per Approval Letter:		

Contract:	Date:
Contractor:	Period From:
Approval Letter:	Period To:
Notes:	Certificate No:

Please pay directly into the following account:

Contractors' Bank Name:	**Account number:**

I.	Original Contract/Work Order Value		1,000,000.00
II.	Approved Variation Orders up to VO #	Net Add/(Deduct)	______
III.	Revised Contract Value (I. + II.)		**1,000,000.00**

				Q.R.
1.	Value of Work Executed Against Original Contract/Work Order			10,000.00
2.	Value of Work Executed Against Site Work Instruction (On Account)			2,000.00
3.	Value of Work Executed Against Approved Formal Variation Orders			1,000.00
A.	**Total Value of Work Executed (1 + 2 + 3)**		Sub-Total	**13,000.00**
4.	Value of Materials on-Site			1,000.00
B.	**Total Value of Work Executed + Materials on-Site (A + 4)**		Sub-Total	**14,000.00**
5.	*Less*: Deduction of Retention	10% of Total Work Executed (item B)	(Deduct)	-1,400.00
6.	*Add*: Release of Retention		Add:	
C.	**Net Value of Work Executed + Materials on-Site (B + 4 + 5)**		Sub-Total	**12,600.00**
7.	*Add*: Advance Payment	10% of Total Original Contract Value (item I)	Add:	100,000.00
8.	*Less*: Recompense Advance Payment	10% of Total Work Executed (Item B)	(Deduct)	-1,400.00
9.	Adjustments per attached tabulation		Add/(Deduct)	
D.	**Value of Work Certified (C + 7 + 8)**		Sub-Total	**111,200.00**
10.	*Less*: Previous Payments No - To		(Deduct)	-1,500.00
E.	**Amount Due This Certificate (D + 9)**		Q.R.	**109,700.00**
	(:)			

For Information Only

F.	Amount Remaining to be Paid Per Revised Contract Value (Item III)	Q.R.	888,800.000

Payment Certified By:

Client	**PM**	**Contractor Agreed**

Sample

19.4 PAYMENT APPLICATION (MILESTONE ACTIVITY COST)

[PROJECT NAME]

Payment Application

Milestone Activity Cost

Contractor: Report Date:

Contract:

Activity ID	Activity Description	Milestone Activity Total cost	Progress	
			(%) Comp.	Due Amount
	Total Contract Price	xxx,xxx,xxx.xx		xxx,xxx,xxx.xx

Grand Total (at last page) xxx,xxx,xxx.xx xxx,xxx,xxx.xx

19.5 COST LOADING SCHEDULE OF VALUES REPORT

[PROJECT NAME]

Cost Loading Schedule of Values Report

Contractor: (1) Report Date: (3)

Contract: (2)

		BOQ Reference		Bill Item		Load			Bill Item	Detailed	Milestone	
Activity ID (4)	Activity Description (5)	Page (6)	Item (7)	Quantity (8A)	Amount (8B)	(%) (9)	Quantity (10A)	Amount (10B)	Description (11)	Activity cost (12A)	Activity cost (12B)	Remarks (15)
	Total Contract Price			xxx,xxx,xxx.xx				xxx,xxx,xxx.xx		xxx,xxx,xxx.xx	xxx,xxx,xxx.xx	

19.6 VARIATION TRACKING LOG

Variation Tracking Log

Project Name :
Project Manager :
Main Consultant :
MEP Consultant :
Main Contractor :
MEP Contractor :

Approval Status	
C	Consultant
PM	Project Manager
PO	Project Owner
N	Not Approved

Legend	
	Mandatory Fields
	As Applicable Fields

Report Date:

Sl. No.	ARF No.	Rev	Description	Amount (AED)	ARF Receipt Date	ARF Approval Date	ARF sent to C&C Date	Date ARF rec'd from C&C	ARF to P Owner Date	ARF from P Owner	ARF to Consult. Date	AVI Receipt Date	AVI to C&C Date	AVI Approval Date	CRF Issue Date	CRF Forward Date	Approval Status	Remarks

19.7 DRAWINGS TRACKING LOG

Drawing Submittal Tracking Log

Project Number:		**Date** 1 Oct-09
Project Name:		**Contractor Details:**
Consultant Details:		**Main:**
Main:		**MEP:**
MEP:		**Other:**
Other:		

Sl.No	Submittal Reference number	Drawing Description	Revision	Planned Subm. Date	Actual Subm-Date	Planned App.Date	Actual App.Date	Approval Code	Required at site Date	Remarks
Structural										
1			0							
			1							
			2							
2			0							
			1							
			2							
Architectural Finishes (Use unique reference and block for each category/finishes contractor)										
1			0							
			1							
			2							
2			0							
			1							
			2							
Coordinated Builder's Work										
1			0							
			1							
			2							
2			0							
			1							
			2							
Coordinated Riser Layouts										
1			0							
			1							
			2							
2			0							
			1							
			2							
Coordinated Reflected Ceiling Layouts										
1			0							
			1							
			2							
2			0							
			1							
			2							
Coordinated Floor tiling Layouts										
1			0							
			1							
			2							
2			0							
			1							
			2							
Coordinated MEP Shop drawings										
1			0							
			1							
			2							
2			0							
			1							
			2							
Coordinated MEP Builder's Work Shop drawings										
1			0							
			1							
			2							
2			0							
			1							
			2							
HVAC										
1			0							
			1							
			2							
2			0							
			1							
			2							
Electrical										
1			0							
			1							
			2							
2			0							
			1							
			2							
Plumbing										
1			0							
			1							
			2							
2			0							
			1							
			2							
Firefighting										
1			0							
			1							
			2							
2			0							
			1							
			2							
DEWA Electricity Load Schedule Approvals										
1			0							
			1							
			2							
2			0							
			1							
			2							
DEWA Water supply and Sewage Approvals										
1			0							
			1							
			2							
2			0							
			1							
			2							
Civil deference Approvals										
1			0							
			1							
			2							
2			0							
			1							
			2							
Etisalat Approvals										
1			0							
			1							
			2							
2			0							
			1							
			2							

Notes:

1. Clause 14 Program of works to be used for extracting planned and required at site dates.
2. Preparation of coordinated contractors shop drawings should be sequenced in tandem after completion of MEP coordination and contractor's shop drawings
3. Fortnightly updates to be submitted on 15th and end of the month.
4. DP will identify drawing submittals requiring PM review

Approval Codes	
A	Approved
B	Approved as noted
C	Reject and resubmit
D	For record

19.8 LONG LEAD ITEM SUBMITTAL AND PROCUREMENT LOG

Pkg. Ref :	
Project name:	
Consultant Details	
Main:	
MEP:	
Other:	

Long Lead Item Submittal and Procurement Tracking Log

Date:	28 Sep-09
Contractor Details	
Main:	
MEP:	
Other:	

Sl.No.	Submittal Reference number	Description	Specified Make	Submitted Make	Local Supplier	Revision	Planned Subm. Date	Actual Subm. Date	Planned App. Date	Actual App. Date	Approval Code	Planned Order date	Actual Order date	Lead time	Planned Del. at site	Exp Del Date	Act. Del. at site	Required at site Date	Remarks
General Items																			
1						0													
						1													
						2													
2						0													
						1													
						2													
Structural																			
1						0													
						1													
						2													
2						0													
						1													
						2													
Architectural Finishes (Use unique reference and block for each category/finishes contractor)																			
1						0													
						1													
						2													
2						0													
						1													
						2													
Mockup/Sample approvals																			
1						0													
						1													
						2													
2						0													
						1													
						2													
HVAC																			
1						0													
						1													
						2													
2						0													
						1													
						2													
Electrical																			
1						0													
						1													
						2													
2						0													
						1													
						2													
Plumbing																			
1						0													
						1													
						2													
2						0													
						1													
						2													
Firefighting																			
1						0													
						1													
						2													
2						0													
						1													
						2													

Notes:

1. Clause 14 Program of works to be used for extracting planned and required at site dates.
2. Fortnightly updates to be submitted on 15th and end of the month.
3. Unpriced purchase order copies with letter of credit details, manufacturer delivery confirmations as applicable to be furnished as per employer request.

Approved Codes	
A	Approved
B	Approved as noted
C	Reject and resubmit
D	For record

19.9 CONSTRUCTION NOC TRACKING LOG

Project Name

Construction NOC and Building Permits

Sl. No.	Service	Authority	Submittal Date		Approval Date		Remarks
			Planned	Actual	Planned	Actual	
1.	Electrical Services	DEWA (Building NOC)					
2.	Electrical Services	DEWA (Substation NOC)					
3.	Water Supply	DEWA					
4.	Telephone Services	DU					
5.	Aircraft Obstruction Study	Dubai Civil Aviation					
6.	Sewerage	TECOM					
7.	Storm water	TECOM					
8.	Irrigation	TECOM					
9.	GSM Services	Etisalat/TECOM					
10.	Fire and Life Safety System	Dubai Civil Defense					
11b	Shoring permit	TECOM					
11c	Piling Building permit	TECOM					
11d	Building permit	TECOM					

19.10 SNAG LIST FORMAT

Snag List

Project Name :
Project Manager :
Main Consultant :
MEP Consultant :
Main Contractor :
MEP Contractor :

Last Updated On :
Last Updated Revision:

Sl. No.	Snag No.	Category	Description	Identification Date	Action By Date	Close-out Date	Contractor Sign-off	Consultant Sign-off	Status	Remarks
Snags										
		STRUCTURAL								
		ARCHITECTURAL								
		MECHANICAL								
		ELECTRICAL								
		OTHER								
Defects										
		STRUCTURAL								
		ARCHITECTURAL								
		MECHANICAL								
		ELECTRICAL								
		OTHER								

19.11 PROJECT HANDING OVER CHECKLIST

Project Handover Checklist

Project Name:		Date:	
Project No.			
Project Manager:			
External Project Manager:			
Consultant:			
Sub-consultant:			
Contractor:			
Sub-contractor:			

	Subject	Content	Required at S.C.	Required within agreed period	Planned Submission Date	Actual Submission Date
A.	Operational Documents	Snag List	☑			
		Technical Training Records	☑			
		Building Furniture List (if applicable)		☑		
		Asset Register (soft copy)		☑		
B.	Operation and Maintenance Manuals	Architectural O&M Manuals		☑		
		Equipment O&M Manuals		☑		
		Equipment Warranties		☑		
		Workmanship Warranties		☑		
		Test and Commissioning Records		☑		
		Manufacturer and Local Agent Details	☑			
		Contractor/Sub-contractor Details	☑			
		Colour Codes (e.g. paint shades, etc.)		☑		
		Spare Parts List		☑		
C.	Building Standards	Design Standards / Project Specs	☑			
D.	Drawings	Approved MEP Shop Drawings	☑			
		Approved Arch. Shop Drawings	☑			
		As Built MEP Drawings		☑		
		As Built Arch. Drawings		☑		
E.	Regulatory Certificates	Civil Defense Certificate	☑			
		Zoning Authority Certificate	☑			
F.	Spare Parts	Spare Parts		☑		
G.	Keys	Keys and Key Boxes	☑			
		Key List	☑			
H.	Building Statistics	Space categories	☑			
		Area calculations	☑			
I.	Other					

Comments:

Glossary

A

Acceptance criteria: Performance requirements and essential conditions that have to be achieved before project deliverables are accepted.

Acceptance test: Formal, pre-defined test conducted to determine the compliance of the deliverable item/s with the acceptance criteria.

Acquisition strategy: Determining the most appropriate means of procuring the component parts or services of a project.

Activity definition: Identifies the specific activities that must be performed in order to produce project deliverables.

Activity ID: A unique code identifying each activity in a project.

Actual cost: Incurred costs that are charged to the project budget and for which payment has been made, or accrued.

Actual cost of work performed (ACWP): Cumulative cost of work accrued on the project in a specific period or upto a specific stage.

Note: For some purposes, cost may be measured in labour hours rather than money.

AND Relationship: Logical relationship between two or more activities that converge on or diverge from an event.

Note: The AND relationship indicates that every one of the activities has to be undertaken.

As-Late-As-Possible (ALAP): An activity for which the early start date is set as late as possible without delaying the early dates of any successor.

As-Soon-As-Possible (ASAP): An activity for which the early start date is set to be as soon as possible. This is the default activity type in most project management systems.

Assumptions: Statements taken for granted or truth.

Audit: Systematic retrospective examination of the whole, or part, of a project or function to measure conformance with pre-determined standards.

Note: Audit is usually qualified, for example financial audit, quality audit, design audit, project audit, health and safety audit.

B

Backward pass: Procedure whereby the latest event times or the latest finish and start times for the activities of a network are calculated.

Balanced matrix: An organizational matrix where functions and projects have the same priority.

Bar Chart: Chart on which activities and their durations are represented by lines drawn to a common time scale.

Note 1: A Gantt chart is a specific type of bar chart and should not be used as a synonym for bar chart.

Note 2: See also 'cascade chart'.

Baseline: Reference levels against which the project is monitored and controlled.

Baseline schedule: The baseline schedule is a fixed project schedule. It is the standard by which project performance is measured. The current schedule is copied into the baseline schedule which remains frozen until it is reset. Resetting the baseline is done when the scope of the project has been changed significantly, for example after a negotiated change. At the point, the original or current baseline becomes invalid and should not be compared with the current schedule.

Benefits management plan: Specifies who is responsible for achieving the benefits set out in the benefits profiles and how achievement of the benefits is to be measured, managed and monitored.

Bottom up cost estimating: This is the method of making estimates for every activity in the work breakdown structure and summarizing them to provide a total project cost estimate.

Brainstorming: The un-structured generation of ideas by a group of people.

Budget: Quantification of resources needed to achieve a task by a set time, within which the task owners are required to work.

Note: A budget consists of a financial and/or quantitative statement, prepared and approved prior to a defined period, for the purpose of attaining a given objective for that period. (The planned cost for an activity or project.)

Budgetary control: System of creating budgets, monitoring progress and taking appropriate action to achieve budgeted performance.

Note: A budget should provide the information necessary to enable approval, authorization and policy-making bodies to assess a project proposal and reach a rational decision.

Budget at completion (BAC): The sum total of the time-phased budgets.

Budgeted cost of work performed (BCWP): The planned cost of work completed to date. BCWP is also the 'earned value' of work completed to date.

Budgeted cost of work scheduled (BCWS): The planned cost of work that should have been achieved according to the project baseline dates.

Business case: Information necessary to enable approval, authorization and policy-making bodies to assess a project proposal and reach a reasoned decision.

C

Change log: A record of all project changes, proposed, authorized, or rejected.

Contingency plan: Mitigation plan. Alternative course(s) of action devised to cope with project risks.

Co-ordinated matrix: An organizational structure where the project leader reports to the functional manager and doesn't have authority over team members from other departments.

Cost benefit analysis: An analysis of the relationship between the costs of undertaking a task or project, initial and recurrent, and the benefits likely to arise from the changed situation, initially and recurrently.

Note: The hard, tangible, readily measurable benefits may sometimes be accompanied by soft benefits which may be real but difficult to isolate, measure and value. (Allows comparison of the returns from alternative forms of investment.)

Cost breakdown structure: Hierarchical breakdown of a project into cost elements.

Cost management: The effective financial control of the project through evaluating, estimating, budgeting, monitoring, analysing, forecasting and reporting the cost information.

Cost performance index (CPI): A measure, expressed as a percentage or other ratio of actual cost to budget plan. (Ratio of work accomplished versus work cost incurred for a specified time period. The CPI is an efficiency rating for work accomplished for resources expended.)

Cost plus fixed fee contract: A type of contract where the buyer reimburses the seller for the seller's allowable costs plus a fixed fee.

Cost plus incentive fee contract (CPIFC): A type of contract where the buyer reimburses the seller for the seller's allowable costs and the seller earns a profit if defined criteria are met.

Cost reimbursement type contracts: A category of contracts based on payments to a Contractor for allowable estimated costs, normally requiring only a 'best efforts' performance standard from the Contractor. Risk for all growth over the estimated value rests with the project owner.

Cost-time resource sheet (CTR): A document that describes each major element in the work breakdown structure, including a statement of work (SOW) describing the work content, resources required, the time frame of the work element and a cost estimate.

Critical path: Sequence of activities through a project network from start to finish, the sum of whose durations determines the overall project duration.

Note: There may be more than one such path. (The path through a series of activities, taking into account interdependencies, in which the late completion of activities will have an impact on the project end date or delay a key milestone.)

Critical path analysis: Procedure for calculating the critical path and floats in a network.

Critical path method (CPM): A technique used to predict project duration by analysing which sequence of activities has the least amount of scheduling flexibility. The critical path method is a modelling process that defines all the project's critical activities which must be completed on time. The start and finish dates of activities in the project are calculated in two phases. The first phase calculates early start and finish dates from the earliest start date forward. The second phase calculates the late start and finish activities from the latest finish date backwards. The difference between the pairs of start and finish dates for each task is the float or slack time for the task. Slack is the amount of time a task can be delayed without delaying the project completion date. By experimenting with different logical sequences and/or durations the optimal project schedule can be determined.

Critical success factor: A factor considered to be most conducive to the achievement of a successful project.

D

Decision event: State in the progress of a project when a decision is required before the start of any succeeding activity.

Note: The decision determines which of a number of alternative paths is to be followed.

Dependency: Precedence relationship. Restriction that one activity has to precede, either in part or in total, another activity. (Dependencies are relationships between products or tasks. For example, one product may be made up of several other 'dependent' products or a task may not begin until a 'dependent' task is complete. See also logical relationship.)

Discounted cash flow (DCF): Concept of relating future cash inflows and outflows over the life of a project or operation to a common base value thereby allowing more validity to comparison of projects with different durations and rates of cash flow.

Duration: The duration of an activity is the time that is required to complete the activity.

E

Earned value: The value of the useful work done at any given point in a project.

Note: The budget may be expressed in cost or labour hours.

Earned value analysis (EVA): Analysis of project progress where the actual money, hours (or other measure) budgeted and spent is compared to the value of the work achieved.

Earned value management: Technique for assessing whether the earned value in relation to the amount of work completed is ahead, on, or behind plan.

Estimate at completion (EAC): A value expressed in either money and/or hours, to represent the projected final costs of work when completed. The EAC is calculated as ETC + ACWP.

Estimate to complete (ETC): The value expressed in either money or hours developed to represent the cost of the work required to complete a task.

F

Fast tracking: Fast tracking is the act of decreasing the overall time required for a project (see schedule compression) without decreasing scope.

Feasibility: The feasibility of a project relates to how likely it is able to be achieved. That is, feasibility relates to how likely the project can implement the stakeholder's requirements within time, financial and other constraints.

Feasibility analysis: The feasibility analysis for a project relates to how likely it is able to be achieved.

Fixed-price contracts: A generic category of contracts based on the establishment of firm legal commitments to complete the required work. A performing Contractor is legally obligated to finish the job, no matter how much it costs to complete. Risks of all cost growth rest on the performing Contractor.

Float: Time available for an activity or path in addition to its planned duration.

(Float is the amount of time that an activity can slip past its earliest completion date without delaying the rest of the project. The calculation depends on the float type.)

Forward pass: A procedure whereby the earliest event times or the earliest start and finish times for the activities of a network are calculated.

Free float: Time by which an activity may be delayed or extended without affecting the start of any succeeding activity.

Note: Free float can never be negative.

G

Gantt chart: Particular type of bar chart showing planned activity against time.

Note: 'Gantt chart', although named for a particular type of bar chart, is in current usage as a name for bar charts in general. (A Gantt chart is a time-phased graphic display of activity durations. Activities are listed with other tabular information on the left side with time intervals over the bars. Activity durations are shown in the form of horizontal bars.)

H

Hammock: Activity, joining two specified points that span two or more activities.

Note 1: Its duration is initially unspecified and is only determined by the durations of the specified activities.

Note 2: Hammocks are usually used to collect time-dependent information, e.g. overheads. (A group of activities, milestones, or other hammocks aggregated together for analysis or reporting purposes. Sometimes used to describe an activity such as management support that has no duration of its own but derives one from the time difference between the two points to which it is connected.)

Hierarchy of networks: Range of networks at different levels of detail, from summary down to working levels, showing the relationships between those networks.

Histogram: A graphic display of planned and/or actual resource usage over a period of time. It is in the form of a vertical bar chart, the height of each bar representing the quantity of resource usage in a given time unit. Bars may be single, multiple, or show stacked resources.

Hypercritical activities: Activities on the critical path with negative float.

I

Internal rate of return (IRR): Discount rate at which the net present value of a future cash flow is zero.

Note: IRR is a special case of the 'discounted cash flow' procedures.

K

Key performance indicators: Measurable indicators that will be used to report progress, which are chosen to reflect the critical success factors of the project.

L

Lag: (a) In a network diagram, the minimum necessary lapse of time between the finish of one activity and the finish of an overlapping activity, (b) Delay incurred between two specified activities.

Latest finish time: The latest possible time by which an activity has to finish within the logical activity and imposed constraints of the network, without affecting the total project duration.

Latest start time: Latest possible time by which an activity has to start within the logical and imposed constraints of the network, without affecting the total project duration.

Lead: In a network diagram, the minimum necessary lapse of time between the start of one activity and the start of an overlapping activity.

Letter of intent: A letter indicating an intent to sign a contract, usually so that work can commence prior to signing that contract.

M

Management by project: A term used to describe normal management processes that are being project managed.

Matrix organization: An organizational structure where the project manager and the functional managers share the responsibility of assigning priorities and for directing the work.

Milestone: A key event. An event selected for its importance in the project.

Note: Milestones are commonly used in relation to progress. (A milestone is often chosen to represent the start of a new phase or the completion of a major deliverable. They are used to monitor progress at summary level. Milestones are activities of zero duration.)

Mission statement: Brief summary, approximately one or two sentences, that sums up the background, purposes and benefits of the project.

Monte Carlo simulation: A technique used to estimate the likely range of outcomes from a complex process by simulating the process under randomly selected conditions a large number of times.

N

Negative total float: Time by which the duration of an activity or path has to be reduced in order to permit a limiting imposed date to be achieved.

Net present value: Aggregate of future net cash flows discounted back to a common base date, usually the present.

Network analysis: Method used for calculating a project's critical path and activity times and floats.

Note: See also critical path analysis, project network techniques.

O

Organizational breakdown structure (OBS): Hierarchical way in which the organization may be divided into management levels and groups, for planning and control purposes.

Original budget: The initial budget established at or near the time a contract was signed or a project authorized, based on the negotiated contract cost or management's authorization.

Overrun: Costs incurred in excess of the contract target costs on an incentive type contract or the estimated costs on a fixed-price contract. An overrun is that value of costs which are needed to complete a project, over that value originally authorized by management.

P

Performance specification: Statement of the totality of needs expressed by the benefits, features, characteristics, process conditions, boundaries and constraints that together define the expected performance of a deliverable.

Note: A performance specification should provide for innovation and alternative solutions, by not defining or unduly constraining the technical attributes of the intended deliverable.

Positive float: Positive float is defined as the amount of time that an activity's start can be delayed without affecting the project completion date. An activity with positive float is not on the critical path and is called a non-critical activity. The difference between early and late dates (start or finish) determines the amount of float.

Post project appraisal: An evaluation that provides feedback in order to learn for the future.

Precedence network: A multiple dependency network. An activity-on-node network in which a sequence arrow represents one of four forms of precedence relationship, depending on the positioning of the head and the tail of the sequence arrow. The relationships are:

(a) Start of activity depends on finish of preceding activity, either immediately or after a lapse of time.

(b) Finish of activity depends on finish of preceding activity, either immediately or after a lapse of time.

(c) Start of activity depends on start of preceding activity, either immediately or after a lapse of time.

(d) Finish of activity depends on start of preceding activity, either immediately or after a lapse of time.

Predecessor: An activity that must be completed (or be partially completed) before a specified activity can begin.

Predecessor activity: In the precedence diagramming method, this is an activity which logically precedes the current activity.

Procurement planning: Determining what to procure and when.

Product breakdown structure: A hierarchy of deliverable products which are required to be produced on the project. It forms the base document from which the execution strategy and product-based work breakdown structure may be derived. It provides a guide for configuration control documentation.

Program management: The effective management of several individual but related projects or functional activities in order to produce an overall system that works effectively.

Project definition: A report that defines a project, i.e. Why it is required? What will be done? How, when and where it will be delivered? The organization and resources required, the standards and procedures to be followed.

Project life cycle: All phases or stages between a project's conception and its termination.

Note: The project life cycle may include the operation and disposal of project deliverables. This is usually known as an 'extended life cycle'.

Project life cycle cost: Cumulative cost of a project over its whole life cycle.

Project management: Planning, monitoring and control of all aspects of a project and the motivation of all those involved in it to achieve the project objectives on time and to the specified cost, quality and performance (Alternative definition—The controlled implementation of defined change).

Project management plan: A plan for carrying out a project, to meet specific objectives, that is prepared by or for the project manager.

Project manager: Individual or body with authority, accountability and responsibility for managing a project to achieve specific objectives.

Project risk management: A sub-set of project management that includes risk identification, risk quantification, risk response development, and risk response control in an effort to identify, analyze and respond to project risks.

Project sponsor

1. The individual or body for whom the project is undertaken, the primary risk taker.
2. The individual representing the sponsoring body and to whom the project manager reports.
3. A person or organization providing funds for the project.

Project success/failure criteria: The criteria by which the success or failure of a project may be judged.

Q

Quality assurance plan: A plan that guarantees a quality approach and conformance to all customer requirements for all activities in a project.

R

Resource: Any variable capable of definition that is required for the completion of an activity and may constrain the project.

Note 1: A resource may be non-storable so that its availability has to be renewed for each time period (even if it was not utilized in previous time periods).

Note 2: A resource may be storable so that it remains available unless depleted by usage. Such a resource may also be replenished by activities producing credited and storable resource. (Resources can be people, equipment, facilities, funding or anything else needed to perform the work of a project.)

Resource smoothing: Scheduling of activities, within the limits of their float, so that fluctuations in individual resource requirements are minimized. (In smoothing, as opposed to resource levelling, the project completion date may not be delayed.)

Responsibility matrix: A document correlating the work required by a work breakdown structure element to the functional organizations responsible for accomplishing the assigned tasks.

Risk: Combination of the probability or frequency of occurrence of a defined threat or opportunity and the magnitude of the consequences of the occurrence.

Note: Combination of the likelihood of occurrence of a specified event and its consequences. (Potential occurrences or threats that would jeopardise the success of a project. The probability of an undesirable outcome.)

Risk analysis: Systematic use of available information to determine how often specified events may occur and the magnitude of their likely consequences. (A technique designed to quantify the impact of uncertainty.)

Risk assessment: The process of identifying potential risks, quantifying their likelihood of occurrence and assessing their likely impact on the project.

Risk avoidance: Planning activities to avoid risks that have been identified.

Risk evaluation: Process used to determine risk management priorities.

Risk management: Systematic application of policies, procedures, methods and practices to the tasks of identifying, analyzing, evaluating, treating and monitoring risk. (The process whereby decisions are made to accept known or assessed risks and/or the implementation of actions to reduce the consequences or probability of occurrence.)

Risk management plan: A document defining how project risk analysis and management is to be implemented in the context of a particular project.

Risk matrix: A matrix with risks located in rows and with impact and likelihood in columns.

Risk transfer: A contractual arrangement between two parties for delivery and acceptance of a product where the liability for the costs of a risk is transferred from one party to the other.

S

Schedule performance index (SPI): Ratio of work accomplished versus work planned, for a specified time period. The SPI is an efficiency rating for work accomplishment, comparing work accomplished to what should have been accomplished.

Scope: The scope is the sum of work content of a project.

Start-to-start lag: Start-to-start lag is the minimum amount of time that must pass between the start of one activity and the start of its successor(s). This may be expressed in terms of duration or percentage.

T

Total float: Time by which an activity may be delayed or extended without affecting the total project duration (or violating a target finish date).

V

Variation: A change in scope or timing of work which a supplier is obliged to do under a contract.

W

What-if analysis: The process of evaluating alternative strategies.

Work breakdown structure (WBS): Way in which a project may be divided by level into discrete groups for programming, cost planning and control purposes.

Note: See also 'work package'. (The WBS is a tool for defining the hierarchical breakdown of work required to deliver the products of a project. Major categories are broken down into smaller components. These are sub-divided until the lowest required level of detail is established. The lowest units of the WBS become the activities in a project. The WBS defines the total work to be undertaken on the project and provides a structure for all project control systems.)

Z

Zero float: Zero float is a condition where there is no excess time between activities. An activity with zero float is considered a critical activity.

References

Amos, Scott J., *Skills and Knowledge of Cost Engineering, Performance and Productivity Management*, Fifth Edition Revised, published in 2007.

Chappell, David, *Building Contract Claims.*

Constre, J., *Contractor's Construction Claim Avoidance.*

——, *Interpretating of Construction Contracts.*

Dilawer, Sayed Ali, *Construction Planning and Scheduling.*

Lewis, *Project Planning and Scheduling.*

Mulcahy, Rita, *PMP Exam Prep-2001*, RMC Publication.

Parker, E. Donald, *Value Engineering Theory*, Revised Edition.

Pickavance, Keith, *Delay and Disruption in Construction Contracts*, Second Edition, published in 2000.

PMBOK Guide, 2000 Edition.

Thiry, Michel, *Value Management Practice.*

Total Cost Management Framework—A Process for Applying the Skill and Knowledge of Cost Engineering, First Edition by AACE International.

